MW01136009

Praise for World Traveler Tales

"Chance Encounters: Travel Tales from Around the World is a delightful collection of stories. Each experience touched and changed the author in some small or large way, all of them significant. The primary drawback of the book is that the tales come to an end. *Chance Encounters* is a good read for every real, as well as armchair, traveler." — *Portland Book Review*

"The stories in *Adventures of a Lifetime* bring out the humorous in encounters with the unfamiliar, show the spirit of adventure that impels the traveler to confront dangers while exploring different cultures, and reveals how understanding broadens with exposure to unknown challenges." — *San Francisco Book Review*

"Each essay in *Chance Encounters: Travel Tales from Around the World* is a glimpse into another life, another time, another place, and reminds us that we are connected in ways we often don't initially recognize." — Author Debbie A. McClure, *TheWriteStuffDotMe*

"*Chance Encounters* ignites my desire to travel, but this spark is only ancillary to the narrative. The real excitement in this collection is not exotic locales, but about connecting to people the world round." — *Amateur Traveler*

World Traveler Tales Books

Chance Encounters: Travel Tales from Around the World (World Traveler Press, 2014)

Adventures of a Lifetime: Travel Tales from Around the World (World Traveler Press, 2015)

A Pink Suitcase: 22 Tales of Women's Travel (World Traveler Press, 2015)

A Pink Suitcase
22 TALES OF
WOMEN'S TRAVEL

Edited by Janna Graber

WORLD TRAVELER PRESS
COLORADO, USA

World Traveler Press
Colorado, USA
www.WorldTravelerPress.com

A Pink Suitcase: 22 Tales of Women's Travel

First edition

ISBN 978-0-9908786-4-3 (Print)
ISBN 978-0-9908786-5-0 (E-book)

"A nomad I will remain for life, in love with distant and uncharted places."

— ISABELLE EBERHARDT

CONTENTS

INTRODUCTION

She was an unusual sight — a middle-aged English woman on horseback, wearing a Hawaiian riding dress, a handkerchief tied over her face and a worn umbrella folded and tied over her hat. Yet, while Isabella Bird was no fashion model, she was determined to go where she wanted — and travel she did.

In 1873, a time when women in the American West were scarce, let alone traveling solo, Bird explored more than 800 miles of rugged canyons, mountain villages and wild mining towns in what was then the Colorado Territory. At times her guide was a one-eyed mountain man who had fallen deeply in love with her, but she had decided he was "a man whom any woman might love but no sane woman would marry," and continued her travels alone.

She often rode her Indian pony Birdie, a plucky beast that carried her where men sometimes feared to tread.

Once during an ice storm, while others stayed inside, Bird simply placed woolen socks on Birdie's hooves for traction and on they went.

Bird wrote of her travels in letters home to her sister. She later collected and published her writings as a book called "A Lady's Life in the Rocky Mountains." Though she didn't know it at the time, Bird was one of America's earliest travel writers, recording a time and place that was quickly fleeting.

I wish I could have met Isabella Bird. I would have loved her passion and would have listened in awe at her stories of travel in India, Japan, China, Korea, Scotland and even the Sandwich Islands (now Hawaii). She is just one of the many women whose curiosity and thirst for knowledge has driven them to explore the world — and inspired me to do the same.

A Pink Suitcase is a collection of remarkable stories from a talented group of modern female explorers. Like Isabella Bird, their tales have delighted and moved me, and I'm pleased to share their adventures with you. Their stories are as diverse as the destinations they traveled to. Some journeyed to the remote corners of the world by sailboat or hiked the Appalachian Trail; others discovered their own hidden strengths when confronting great challenges, dangers or even loss. Several women simply took up the challenge of trying something new because they could – and did! – reveling in the joy of accomplishment and fresh discoveries. Still others found healing in travel, a soothing balm when nothing else seemed to help.

They traveled as mothers, sisters, wives, daughters, friends and lovers. Sometimes they traveled alone, whether by choice or circumstance, often forming deep connections with the people who crossed their paths. Many learned that curiosity, courage and sometimes even a sense of humor can create an experience that is not only unforgettable, but also transforming.

I find it ironic that most of the explorers I learned about in school were men, yet I am most inspired by women who travel not only for pleasure, but for the joy and reward it brings, even when that reward comes with difficulties.

It was a woman who first introduced me to the wonder of travel. My college roommate Melanie had been to Europe the summer before my sophomore year, and after class each day she'd tell me story after story of handsome Dutch boys, vibrant European cities and fascinating cultures. Eventually, she wore me down and off we went — two American girls just out of their teens on the ultimate European road trip.

The two weeks that we spent driving through the continent (driving! - what were we thinking?) were magical and transforming. After returning, I packed my bags and told my parents I was off to Europe. Now that I'm a mom myself, I can see what courage it must have taken for my parents to let me go. Yet they encouraged me to follow my dream, patiently listening whenever I called home during the next two years from post offices across Europe.

Travel has continued to be a big part of my life, as well as the lives of my family. I took my firstborn to Europe when she was only 5 months old, carrying her close in a front pack as I walked the cobblestone streets of Vienna. Over the years we've explored towns from Sydney to Oslo, and my children (there were soon three of them) became adept at pulling their own little suitcases.

Some of the most touching experiences came when I took one child alone on a trip. Outside of our normal lives and sibling dynamics, I could see a new side of that child that was often masked. "Thailand's Lost Children," my own story in this book, is one such example.

I'm not the only mother who has wanted to introduce their children to the rewards of travel. In *A Pink Suitcase*, a mother's determination and love for her child knows no bounds as she scours the Chinese countryside hoping to uncover her daughter's past, while another is determined to overcome every obstacle to give her daughter her dream trip to Paris.

I'm not sure if wanderlust is genetic or simply learned, but one day I became the mother sitting across from her daughter while she spoke of her travel plans and moving overseas. My throat ached as I watched my middle daughter pack her bags and book her tickets. As we drove her to the airport, I could already feel the weight of her empty room.

"It's just for a year mom," she told me as she skipped into the airport. "And now we have Skype and email. I can tell you all about it!"

Yes, indeed. Just like the women in this book, we all have to find our own way in the world, whether in the steamy climes of French Polynesia, on a sailboat somewhere in the Pacific or in our own hometowns. For years, I have treasured reading and telling the stories of travel. Now it was time for my daughter to create travel stories of her own.

Janna Graber is the editor of two other World Traveler Press anthologies — Chance Encounters: Travel Tales from Around the World and Adventures of a Lifetime. She is an American travel journalist, editor and producer who has covered travel in more than 38 countries. She fell in love with travel while studying abroad in Austria, and has been hooked ever since. Janna is the managing editor and founder of GoWorldTravel.com. Read more of her work at jannagraber.com or follow her on Twitter @AColoradoGirl.

A Pink Suitcase
22 TALES OF
WOMEN'S TRAVEL

THE HUMAN RACE
French Polynesia

I'm crouched at the starting line at 4:30 a.m., stretching tentatively, my palms indented with loose bits of asphalt, feeling twitchy. It's still dark, the stars hidden beneath cloud cover. Already 84 degrees. With humidity running well above 80 percent, it feels like the mid-90s though the sun has not even begun to rise. Not an ideal day to run the 21 kilometers (13.1 miles) of a *semimarathon*, as it's called here in French Polynesia, especially for someone used to running in the arid climate of Southern California, but that seems to be what I'm about to do.

Half an hour ago I watched as participants in the full marathon took off when the air horn blew. Many of them looked like runners I'm used to back home in Los Angeles: iPods strapped to upper arms, waists garlanded with energy packs and electrolyte goo, legs striated with sinewy muscle, singlets sporting competitor numbers hanging slack on slender torsos. Most wore regular-looking running shoes; more than a few ran barefoot.

Now the rest of us are clumped together waiting our turn an hour after the full marathon's departure. I'm nervous. This will be the first race I've run without my running partner Emily. ("Trot" is actually a more accurate verb for what we do, "run" being a little too ambitious.) I'm in a foreign country where I don't speak the language, about to run a race I haven't trained for, amid weather conditions that are utterly unfamiliar and punishing to my body.

Why, dear God, did I sign up to do this?

Three weeks ago I moved to the village of Pao Pao on the island of Moorea in the South Pacific. (Look at a globe. Put your finger on Hawaii, and then drop it down, down, down, half a world away directly to the south. See those microscopic dots floating between South America and Australia? I'm on one of those.) I'll be here three months, living with my brother Frank and his Tahitian family of six. The people speak French and Tahitian. I know only English and a smattering of Spanish. Most are dark-haired and bronze-skinned. With red hair and freckles, I don't quite fit in.

But I'm hoping there's a place for me somewhere here on the island of Moorea, and that in finding it, I might also find my place in the larger world. In my own life.

The question of what I'm doing in French Polynesia in the first place is hard to answer. There's the pat response: I'm on sabbatical from the university here, where I teach creative writing, to write a book. Sounds ideal. But the truth is stickier. I'm here in many ways to lick my wounds, having left a marriage of 25 years and started my life anew as a solo voyage a year-and-a half ago. It feels like I've run at least 20 marathons in that time just surviving the challenges and upsets, learning how to hang in no matter what. Back in LA, I live in a studio apartment over a garage; a life that used to fill 2,000 suburban square feet shared with three kids, a dog and husband has been pared back, stripped away one shred at a time, until it's just me, tender at the bone, fitting into 400 city square feet.

When my youngest left for university this past fall, the all-consuming child-rearing portion of my life came to a bittersweet end, leaving me to figure out who I was and where I was going.

Over the past two years, my life has been blasted to bits, much at my own hand. My father died. I left my marriage. I learned to ride a motorcycle and bought a Harley. I got tattooed. I rode my motorcycle across the country. I went backpacking and open-water kayaking and mountain climbing and marathon running. And now I'm staying on a tropical island many people call Paradise, trying to make sense of it all. My ex would tell you I'm having a midlife crisis. But it's more than that. And though friends and colleagues think I'm here indulging in an extended vacation highlighted by fruit-rich drinks served in coconut shells by handsome cabana boys in the languid post-swim/post-yoga afternoon, the truth is different. And I knew it would be when I bought the plane ticket.

Many days I take in my surroundings as if I'm inside some kind of tropical snow globe. Lagoons and bays of transparent blue-green water, coconut trees, sandy beaches, coral reefs and lushness surround me. Yet my life is in shambles. I sit and stare at the bay as bits of snow-like debris from the self-inflicted agitation settle, hoping I'll recognize a path forward when I can finally see objectively again.

I had no idea, for example, that a *semimarathon* would be part of the deal.

In the three weeks I've been here, the challenges have been epic. I live in a house open to the elements — think the Swiss Family Robinson tree house, minus the tree. The house sports a roof and low walls that rise from the foundation to waist level, but between the low walls and the roof everything is open, the great outdoors given full access, vegetation creeping its way in. Geckos scale my bedroom walls and click at me at night, freaking me out. Insects are at home here, as is the occasional wild chicken that flies into the house by mistake, an experience I don't particularly care for. Feral dogs congregate outside my bedroom, hoping for scraps, and a 150-piece rooster orchestra breaks into song every morning at 3 o'clock. It's hard to shower without being bitten by the countless mosquitoes that like to hang out there.

The rains came the second week I was here. Eight days of nonstop torrents so loud I had trouble having a conversation for the noise. The turquoise bay filled with runoff from the pineapple plantations until the entire Cook's Bay (named for explorer Capt. James Cook) looked as if it was filled with chocolate milk. This was not the tropical paradise I had been promised. Meanwhile, everything in the open-air house — sheets, towels, every last shred of clothing, pillows, you name it — became dank and smelled of mildew. Clothes could not be washed because there was no way to dry them. My belt grew a fur coat one day that, when washed off, came back the next. I climbed into damp sheets at night, put my head on a damp pillow and wished for Vicks VapoRub to put under my nose to replace the clammy, mildew stink. Those were the nights I wanted to cry myself to sleep, but I dared not for fear of insulting my brother and his family. They're doing all they can to make my time here pleasant; it's just so foreign.

And I'm so broken.

Meanwhile, my legs have taken on a leprous look, thanks to the intense reaction I'm having to the mosquito, no-see-um and other insect bites. My sister-in-law sewed me a mosquito net that is both gorgeous and functional. (There are no Targets here, no stores to run out and get what you need. You go to the market each afternoon to see what's available for dinner, and whatever's there, those are your choices. If there's no fish, you pick something else. No tomato sauce, no spaghetti tonight.

You need something like a mosquito net, you make it. And as long as you're going to make it, you might as well make it beautiful. Even the light poles are festooned with flowers and coconut palms woven by anyone in the mood, the desire for beauty deeply ingrained in all Tahitians. Oh, what I hope to learn from these people!)

Little by little I am grasping, as if by Braille, new ways of being. One night, Frank asked if I knew how to make pizza. Aware their kitchen had limitations, I first queried him: "You have measuring cups, a rolling pin, a board to roll out dough on, pizza pans?"

"Yeah, yeah. Let's just get the ingredients," he said. When we got home the truth came out. "I lied," he said, "but I'm sure you can figure it out."

Using drinking glasses as measuring cups, an old wine bottle as a rolling pin, the table itself as a rolling surface and large pans never intended for pizza, I struggled. Whatever I created was sure to be a disappointment. How could it not, under these conditions? I did my best. The dough rose miraculously, then rolled out to just the right size for the three extra-large pizzas I was constructing. The first one exited the oven to oohs and ahhs of my impressed nieces and nephews. Everyone sat around the dinner table, expectant. Maybe my efforts would pay off, after all. I felt a little bubble of happiness rise in my chest.

But then the oven, which doesn't seem to have any temperature settings, started to lose heat. Perhaps the propane was gone? As the night progressed, the second two pizzas sat in the oven, trying and failing to cook. We ate the first pizza — not nearly enough for seven people — and fed the doughy second two to the wild dogs.

What I haven't learned yet is how to fully belong.

Having left my own family, I feel at times like an intruder with my brother's family, as if, in giving up mine I've given up the right to belong to a family at all. Plus there's all the history. Frank is older by more than four years. When growing up, we both struggled to help raise our younger three siblings in the shadow of our mother's severe mental illness. He adopted a stance of impenetrability, a "can-do" attitude that I tried to emulate, but often failed. At university, where he couldn't afford the dorm fees, he simply set up a tent in the redwood forest surrounding the school, showered in the gym and studied in the library. He has little patience for the rest of us who are not quite as capable as he is.

When the rains started here, he gave me the keys for a small truck. The vehicle had no power steering, reverse gear was located in a different place than I was used to, and the road to the house had become a muddy stone-lodged river that begged for four-wheel drive, which this vehicle did not have. After I drove it home one night, terrified I'd get stuck, I told him the next morning I'd prefer waiting for the rains to let up rather than continue driving it.

"Oh, come on!" Aggravation made his voice into a bark. "We grew up in the same house. If I can figure out this stuff, so can you!" I sulked for a bit, until minutes later when his adult step-daughter got her car stuck in the very patch I had feared. With Frank's four-wheel-drive truck and a lot of cursing, we extracted her car. I was sorry she got stuck but was glad I'd held my ground.

Still, the old impulses remain. This is the brother I looked up to as a child, whom I adored and wanted to be like. He was a star on the high school swim and water polo teams. I floundered in that same pool, trying and failing to make my mark. In college, he pursued marine biology. I tried to follow suit until I failed chemistry. It's painful to admit — both then and now — that I'm often unable to live up to his desires for me, or even my own desires for myself. And yet, the discomfort is easing. I'm learning to tease him — the lion whom, as a child, I would never dare taunt — and we're getting comfortable with each other.

He gave me crap the other night when, serving as his sous chef, I asked how he wanted the broccoli and car-rots chopped. "For God's sake. Make a decision. Chop the damn things!" Instead of moping, I gave him back as good as I got. His family rallied to my side.

"Hey, it's been decades since we lived with each oth-er," he said, defending himself from the onslaught of support given me. "I have a lot of shit-giving to make up for." We all laughed — a genuine laugh, not the "can't you take a joke?" kind. Something is healing.

In packing to come here, I brought my running gear with the thought that I'd go for the occasional trot. The heat and humidity have forced me to scale back my normal 10K jaunts and walk a lot. When I heard about the marathon to be held on this little island, I knew I couldn't possibly be ready in time. And then I reconsidered. If I lowered my expectations, did only the *semimarathon* and gave myself permission to walk as much as needed, perhaps I could. My niece helped me sign up. A doctor's physical was required, so I navigated the medical system with her, conversing stiltedly with a French doctor, and registered to run. Last night, I walked down the dirt-and-rock road from the house alone in the dark, a headlamp lighting my way, to attend the runners' Pre-Race Pasta Party.

My heart thumped as I checked in without a family member to translate. I showed my bib number and the woman figured it out. I sat at a table, eating my pasta alone, watching the Polynesian dancers and fire-eaters do their thing. All around me, people spoke French and Tahitian. I felt like an outsider, one who will never belong.

This morning, I woke at 3:30, dressed in the dark and used the headlamp to light my way to the starting line. A man in a pickup truck passed me and shouted "*Bon Marathon!*" A smile split my face.

Maybe I'm wrong. Maybe I'm learning to belong after all.

At the check-in table, I showed my number and joined the other racers drinking water and eating snacks.

One asked me if I knew where the *toilette* was. I shook my head mutely.

Now, at the starting line, the officials are giving out information about the race and I have no idea what they're saying. But I get the general gist and follow the rest of the runners as we move down the road, closer to where they want us to start. Huddled together, I see a man wearing a shirt from "A Runner's Circle," the little running shop from my Los Feliz neighborhood in LA. This flimsy connection to home suddenly makes him seem like a long-lost relative; I want to hug him. Instead, I touch him gingerly on the shoulder. "Do you speak English?" He shakes his head. I point first at his shirt and then at me, trying to pantomime the significance. He nods, smiles.

Eventually the air horn blasts and we take off in a pack. Less than a mile into the race, we pass the intersection of the little dirt road that leads to my brother's house. I'm surprised to the point of tears to see Frank, his wife and my nephew standing on the roadside at 5 a.m. cheering me. The path I've been on this past two years has felt so lonely, so void of familial support. When I first left my marriage, my sister said, "You can't expect to do something like that and not have people be mad at you." Another brother said nothing. So now, to have family — especially my older brother — standing here in the pre-dawn light cheering for me is amazing. And humbling.

I find my stride and settle in. Water stations appear every 2.5 kilometers, but instead of offering simply drinking water, they also provide gloriously wet sponges that you squeeze over your head and body to cool off. There's no Gatorade or Powerade, but occasionally fruit juice is offered or cut-up bits of pineapple and papaya. We run and the sun begins to rise, painting the bay in peaches and pinks.

The route runs parallel to the island shore so we're always within spitting distance of the ocean. The view is stunning. Families have come to the roadside to cheer. Some yell "Go! Go!" in French: "*Alle, madame!*" Others shout don't-give-up encouragement in Tahitian: "*Faitoi-to.*" By 7K, I'm feeling weak, but don't berate myself. I didn't come here to set any personal best. I came to join my sweat with others, to be part of something bigger than myself. The day heats up and the sponges are not nearly as frequent as I'd like, but my legs keep moving forward.

When I hit the 11-kilometer mark and stop for a sponge, I'm almost knocked over by the leader of the full marathon as he laps me and grabs for his own sponge. "*Pardon! Pardon!*" he shouts, trying to right me as he runs on.

Soon, other marathoners are lapping me. I don't care. Small groups of Tahitian musicians have gathered to sing the runners forward. A clump of drummers drives up and down the road in an open-air truck, thrumming out a beat to keep us moving. Onward! I'm in the swim of humanity now. Just a runner among runners. Not American. Not English-speaking, just another human.

As I approach the finish line, a marathoner comes up from behind me moving at a good clip. How he knows I only speak English, I have no idea. "Come on. You and me," he says with a French accent. "We'll finish together." I rally and try to match his stride, but lose him a hundred feet before the finish. Still, I did it. I finished the race. Frank and my nephew are at the finish line, cheering. The volunteers garland my neck with leis of fresh flowers and seashells. I am given my "finisher's" T-shirt.

Back home after the race, I fall deeply, satisfyingly asleep. I have done something profoundly important. I have tried, literally, to join the human race, to add my puny bit of effort to those of the people with whom I find myself living. My niece will show me two days hence that I finished 350th out of a field of 358. It doesn't matter where I finished, only that I was part of it.

In the weeks to come, I will learn a few things: I will learn that a *pāreu*, a rectangular piece of colorful fabric, can be made to function as a dress, a skirt, a shawl to keep the sun off, or a towel to lie on at the beach and with which to dry oneself off after a swim. I will learn how to wield a squash-size racket-looking device that electrocutes mosquitoes while simultaneously carrying on a dinner conversation. I will learn that stale bread gets chucked from the dinner table into the yard for the wild chickens and dogs to appreciate. (And though it's called a yard, the land is much wilder than that suburban image elicits, more like a rain forest.) I will learn how to eat rambutan, a spiny red fruit that's similar to lychee, how to buy fruit and roast chicken and whole raw fish from vendors set up on folding tables along the main road, how to know which food scraps to add to the worms in the compost bin, which go in the trash, and which are put out for the animals.

I will learn to say hello, goodbye, please, and thank you in both Tahitian and French. How to go to the store early each morning for the freshly-baked baguettes that are a breakfast staple. How to make *poisson cru*, raw fish similar to ceviche in which the fish is first "cooked" in lime juice, then mixed with tomatoes, onion, cucumber and freshly squeezed coconut milk. I will learn the difference between coconut water and coconut milk and how to get each. I will learn through painful experience how to eradicate the fungus that grows on the bottom of the toes, splitting the skin where the toes join the foot, and how to squeeze fresh lime onto a wound when you cut yourself on the coral reef. I will learn that my older brother loves me and likes having me as part of his family. And that I can start the process of belonging any time I want to.

Bernadette Murphy writes about literature, women, risk-taking and life — from motorcycles to knitting — and has published three books, including the best-selling

"Zen and the Art of Knitting." Her fourth book, "Look, Lean, Roll: A Woman, A Motorcycle and Plunging into Risk," will be published by Counterpoint Press in spring 2016. She is an associate professor in the Creative Writing Department of Antioch University Los Angeles. A former weekly book critic for the Los Angeles Times, her essays on life and literature have appeared in Ms. magazine, Los Angeles Times Magazine, San Francisco Chronicle, The Oregonian, San Jose Mercury News, Newsday, BOOK magazine, and elsewhere. She holds a MFA from Antioch University and is the mother of three young adults. Her website is bernadette-murphy.com.

WALK IN THE WOODS
Canada

I was several hours by foot from the nearest town, deep into the backcountry of Canada's Jasper National Park, when I saw it. The small mass of brown fur scampered down the hillside toward me at an alarming speed.

"Animal!" I squealed to my companions. In my panic, I couldn't even form the words to describe the creature I thought was running toward me: A grizzly bear cub that no doubt would be followed by its very large, very protective, probably very likely-to-eat-my-face-off mother.

You can get a good sense of what people think of you by their reaction to your travel plans. So maybe I should have been concerned when the responses to the news of my latest trip were surprise, worry and even outright laughter. I was embarking on a three-day, 27-mile hike in the grizzly-bear-infested wilds of the Canadian Rockies. An out-of-shape, neurotic, tech-addicted, admittedly prissy city dweller, I am the last person you'd expect to attempt an adventure such as this. And that was really the point.

"Were you drinking when you signed up for this?" my mom asked, once she stopped laughing. "Why would you want to do this?" asked one friend on Facebook. Another simply commented, "Hahahaha." The jokes increased once I explained that the women-only guided hike offered by a company called Skyline Adventures was dubbed "The Gutsy Girl Adventure."

If you're signing up for something that labels you as a "gutsy girl," chances are you are not one, a fact that became clearer as the date of my impending adventure drew near. I had cajoled my friend, Annemarie, into joining me on the trip, figuring that she and I would be on equal footing. Annemarie is a born-and-bred New Yorker and, I assumed, would be as unqualified for the trip as I was.

I quickly started to worry I might have assumed wrong. When Annemarie texted me photos of the lanterns and first-aid kits she was considering packing, I sent back photos of REI's selection of outdoor wine glasses and lightweight wine pouches. While she shopped for mini camping axes, I bought a travel-sized hairbrush.

As the trip drew nearer — and Annemarie flooded my inbox with more pictures of the hike's highest point, the Notch, which she'd pulled from Instagram searching the Skyline Trail hashtag — I became more certain that I would be the weak link on this hike.

However, when we met in Edmonton for the train ride to Jasper, some of my fears were calmed. As I worried about where we'd go to the bathroom in the woods, Annemarie wondered if we'd have cell service and how often she could update social media. I detailed the contents of my bag — several pairs of hiking pants, a fleece, multiple pairs of wool socks, a poncho, a headlamp — and found that Annemarie's list of necessities was much shorter: a jacket, a pair of jeans, glow sticks, several rolls of toilet paper and two boxes of Band-Aids.

I typed out a Twitter post and read it aloud: @Annemarie brought glow sticks, but no pants. Apparently she thought we were going to Burning Man in the woods.

Annemarie laughed. "I'm also planning to live-blog this whole thing. You brought an extra cell charger, right?" I felt a bit of relief course through me — I might be sorely unqualified for this hike, but at least Annemarie was too.

The morning of our hike I repacked all my gear into my behemoth of a backpack, brushed my hair, put on makeup and posed for what I assumed would be the only decent photo of me for the duration of the trip.

Facebook post: Off to hike in the woods. Do I look like a wilderness girl?

At 8 a.m., our guide, Sarah, picked us up for the short drive to the trail's end, where we'd meet her friend,

Christian, leave Sarah's car, and then catch a ride to the start of the trail. Along the way, Sarah directed our attention out the window. "That's where we're going. That's the Notch."

Nausea set in immediately. The Notch, a depression between two snow-capped peaks, seemed to loom miles above us.

"*That's* the Notch?" Annemarie asked, incredulous. "What kind of a pervert would climb that?"

"I guess us," I replied.

Instagram post: Here's a pic of the mountain we're about to climb. Yes, we're idiots.

#teamperverts

At the trailhead Christian helped us adjust our packs. "Wow," he said, lifting mine onto my back, "that's heavy. What do you have in there?" I detailed my supplies, though I neglected to mention the half bottle of wine I'd portioned into a plastic platypus bag.

#priorities

"Come on," Annemarie said, once we were fully adjusted and had snapped a photo of us beaming in front of the trail sign. "Are you ready to go cry in the woods and talk about our feelings?"

Facebook post: Into the woods!

#reenacting*Wild*

Once the post published, I switched off the connection on my phone. Crushing Annemarie's plans for liveblogging our adventure, Sarah had told us there was no cell service on the trail. As of this moment, we'd have no connection to the outside world for the next three days. Forget the Notch, I thought. This might be the hike's biggest challenge.

The day started out easy enough, through shady forest with only the slightest incline, but still my shoulders and back ached under the weight of my pack. It was much heavier than I'd anticipated, and I began to worry how I was going to make it through all three days if it hurt this bad after just a few hours. Then Sarah gave me something more important to worry about: grizzly bears.

There are more than 100 grizzly bears living in Jasper National Park and they sometimes cross paths with hikers, so Sarah had supplied us each with a canister of bear spray.

"Do we just spray it around our tents?" Annemarie asked.

"I don't think it's bear-repellent," I replied. "I think it's more like bear mace."

Sarah nodded, but added that it was a last resort. The canisters hold only about 8 seconds worth of spray, with a reach of just six feet. But Sarah assured us that it likely wouldn't come to that. A better line of defense, she said, was to make enough noise that bears stayed away. If we did see a bear, we should keep our eyes down and try to appear nonthreatening. If the bear didn't immediately move on, we should simply try saying "go away bear," a phrase that had proven successful for Sarah over the years. I was skeptical.

"Bears don't really want to mess with you," Sarah assured us, though she stressed that we should carry bear spray at all times — on the trail, in our tents and while using the bathroom — and we should travel together whenever possible.

Annemarie shook her head. "Bears are out there and looking to kill," she countered. "I think they are checking Facebook and the Skyline Trail hashtag. They're tech-savvy and they will find us. "

I decided to practice my aim with the bear spray.

After lunch, the trail began its first big climb. As we ascended above the treeline, views of the sun-dappled mountains that encircle the trail opened around us. Early in the hike, I'd decided to take photos of every mile of the trail — or at least what felt like every mile. By 3 p.m., when we began the descent to our campground on the valley floor, I was taking photos every few minutes.

By the time we made it to camp we were exhausted, but there was still work to do before we could relax. First, Sarah showed us how to set up our tent and how to filter drinking water to replenish the two liters we'd consumed throughout the day.

After dinner, she pulled out a map to show us how far we'd come, and how far we still had to go. The next day would be much harder than the first. We'd cover a gradual ascent of five miles in the morning, stop for lunch at a lake, and then tackle the hardest part of the hike — the steep ascent to the Notch. The Notch, a ridge at more than 8,000 feet, was the highest point on the trail.

After we made it to the top, we'd have to hike several more hours before reaching camp. Noticing our looks of concern — possibly panic, in my case — Sarah added that if we weren't up to it or if the weather turned foul, there were several alternate routes we could take that would deviate onto other trails.

At camp, we were joined by a group of college-age men who seemed far too energetic to have hiked the same eight miles we'd covered, as well as a young Norwegian woman who was tackling the hike solo. She'd already hiked similar trails in the Alps and the Andes on her own. Like Sarah, she was a true "gutsy girl," while I was just playing one.

That night, we also met Mr. Lumpy — the official name given to the structure that passed for an open-air "bathroom" at each camp — a rickety wooden platform over a plastic five-gallon bucket. At each camp it was inevitably located back in the woods, far away from the tents, so Annemarie and I decided to visit in pairs.

While Annemarie stood guard, holding her bear spray at the ready and calling out, "no bears, go away bears," I balanced over the makeshift toilet's rim, clutching my own bear spray in one hand and toilet paper in the other, and constantly swiveling my head around to look for the bears I assumed were hiding in the shadows waiting to pounce while I was at my most vulnerable.

Before I traded positions with Annemarie, I snapped a quick selfie standing in front of Mr. Lumpy. I decided that if I survived this trip, I'd need proof of the many challenges I'd overcome along the way.

#roughingit

Back at camp, Annemarie's glowsticks proved more valuable than my blindingly bright headlamp. The pink and purple sticks softly illuminated the tent in the growing dark. It was only 8 p.m., but I was having trouble staying awake and my back ached as though it was still carrying my heavy pack.

"It feels like I'm still wearing my backpack," I whined to Annemarie as I tried out different positions. "It's like phantom limb, but worse. It's phantom backpack." I felt more tired than I ever had in my life.

"OK, quick picture and then you can sleep," Annemarie said, grabbing her phone. We each grinned and held a glowstick triumphantly aloft as Annemarie snapped a few shots. Within minutes, I was asleep.

#tentparty

The next morning, we shouldered our heavy packs at 8 a.m. and set out on a four-hour hike through a flower-filled meadow. Beyond the cobalt blue lake that would be our lunch stop, the trail became a faint, jagged line that seemed to run vertically up the mountain. The ascent was so steep, Sarah guessed it would take us nearly two hours to reach the Notch and, once there, we'd still have seven miles of hiking ahead.

"It's going to be really hard," she said, "and there are times you are going to be really scared, but you will not fall. You just need to trust your feet." If we didn't feel up to it, she reminded us, we could change our route, but once we reached a certain point on the ascent, there was no turning back.

My pack, stuffed with 30 pounds of supplies and the hefty weight of self-doubt, pulled on my shoulders and dug into my hips. My thighs shook with the fatigue of the morning's ascent, my feet ached, and a familiar sour lump hit the back of my throat as my eyes welled with tears of exhaustion. We were 12 miles from the start of the hike, 15 miles from its end, and far away from my comfort zone.

With some doubt in my mind, I committed to the attempt.

As Sarah predicted, the climb was hard; with each step my pack seemed to get heavier as I labored up the trail, sliding on loose scree, wobbling on unstable rocks, or shoving my toes into crude stairs dug into the steepest parts. When the trail narrowed to the width of my foot and tilted toward a long plunge down the mountainside, I remembered Sarah's assurance that I wouldn't fall. Her instructions to trust my feet became a mantra, repeated with each unsteady step.

Each time I stopped to gasp for air or rest my shaking muscles, I could see the lake below shrinking smaller, as the views of the silver-tipped mountains expanded all around us. Finally, we reached the top. I should have been exhilarated, but I was exhausted. After the effort, the thought of covering seven more miles made me want to cry.

The only sound was the wind, and my own heavy breathing. And then, "Instagram!" Annemarie yelled suddenly, waving her phone in the air. "Instagram! People posted photos on Instagram and tagged this location. That means there's cell service here!"

I toggled my phone off of airplane mode and watched as the bars of service blinked back to life and the phone's icons counted the messages I'd received in the last 30 hours.

There were texted notes of encouragement, tweets from friends and messages from my husband saying how proud of me he was, and that he was sure I was doing fine. I started to feel giddy as I scrolled through them. I wasn't sure if it was the emotional boost from messages of friends and family rooting for me or simply the lack of oxygen to my brain, but I suddenly felt like I could do anything. The next seven miles no longer worried me. I texted a quick note to my husband and posted a photo of Annemarie and I smiling high above the trail below, sharing it to Facebook, Instagram and Twitter with the push of a button.

#wemadeit

During our brief celebration, indigo clouds had gathered above so it wasn't long before Sarah herded us onward down the trail, and back out of cell range. We were far above the tree line and completely exposed to the elements — not a place we wanted to be in a storm. As tiny shards of hail pelted our packs, we hustled along the barren ridgeline and then back down to the valley floor and our camp for the night.

The next morning I woke up energized. We had only eight miles left, and most of it was downhill. Over breakfast, we celebrated how far we'd come, and I lamented that I was almost disappointed that we didn't see a bear. "From far away," I quickly clarified.

"Actually," Sarah responded, "this is the campground where I usually see them. One morning two big males even tried to join us for breakfast. From here to the trail's end is all grizzly habitat, so you still might have a chance to see one."

As we packed up camp, Annemarie and I held our bear spray close at hand. I kept up my vigilance out on the trail too, at least at first. Eventually, I became caught up in the views and daydreaming about the cold beer that was waiting for me in just a few miles.

And that's when I saw it. The brown ball of fur that I was certain was a ferocious grizzly cub with razor-sharp claws. I didn't even have time to fumble for my bear spray or to scream the name of the animal I thought was about to attack.

Before I could process what I was really looking at, my panic was interrupted by Sarah and Annemarie doubled over in laughter.

The ferocious grizzly bear cub was a marmot.

I swallowed my embarrassment and focused on the chubby rodent as it slowed to a waddle. When it paused to sniff the ground a few yards from my feet, I crouched down and stretched my hand in the marmot's direction. "It's cute," I said. "Can I make friends with it?"

"Sure," Sarah replied. "They're harmless. Well except some of them carry the plague...."

I settled for a photo of Annemarie posing a few feet from it.

Instagram post: Making new friends.

#plaguemarmots

Three hours later, we reached the bottom of the trail. At the sight of the parking lot we all cheered with relief. We stopped for a photo at the sign marker for the trail's end — photographic proof of our success — and then headed back to town where hot showers and cold beers awaited.

Facebook post: We're done! Maybe we're not gutsy girls, but we faced down wild animals and conquered a mountain. We even survived nearly three days without cell phones. I think that might be gutsy enough for me.

Katie Hammel has written about travel, food and wine for BBC Travel, travelandleisure.com, AOL Travel, San Francisco Chronicle, Maxim, Conde Nast Traveler, The Points Guy and New York Daily News.Born in Detroit, she lived in Seattle and Chicago before settling in San Francisco with her husband and two fat cats. She loves California cabernet, hates running but does it anyway, and believes the West Coast is the best coast. She dreams of one day living on a farm in Iceland.

STARS AND A STRANGER
India

In Ladakh, India, night falls fast after the sun drops below the mountain horizon. Before I've walked just a few hundred yards past the town center, I'm enveloped in a blackness that's as total and soft as a velvet shroud. No streetlights, no moon to light the dusty path. No flashlight, either.

I slow my pace, sliding my sandaled feet along the dirt ruts made by the yak carts. Then I glance upward and see the stars. Freed from the garish glare of civilization, they glow unabashedly. Not enough to illuminate my way back to the hotel, but enough to inspire awe. Where do I end and the stars begin? I don't know, but here in a Himalayan valley along the Indus River, I relax and feel at peace.

Suddenly my hand brushes against a person walking in silence beside me. With a start, I remember that I'm not alone in a benign universe. I'm walking beside a man from Afghanistan I met only two hours ago. We're on a deserted road. The town of Leh, capital of Ladakh, is shuttered behind me, the hotel whose name I've forgotten somewhere up ahead.

My heart pounds like a tabla drum as my vulnerability sinks in. The fellow seemed sweet enough in his jewelry shop, even gallant, but I wouldn't have accepted his offer to escort me back to my hotel had I any idea that twilight didn't exist here. I should have known, given that India is a nation of brilliant colors and high contrasts: jewel-encrusted, silk-adorned wealth beside dung-stinking, fly-swarming poverty. There are no pastels in India. Why shouldn't night follow day without the middle hues of dusk?

I pretend I'm dreaming and will wake up safe in day's reassuring light. My sandal strikes a sharp stone on the road and punctures my pretensions. Fear sears my insides. This is real.

I'm alone with stars and a stranger.

How did I let myself borrow trouble? It started when I signed up for a low-cost tour of northern India and Nepal that was going to places I had dreamed of and whose names had the rhythms of poetry: Katmandu, Srinagar, Varanasi, Khajuraho, Agra, Ladakh.

Ladakh District was as close as I could get, geographically and spiritually, to Tibet. The itinerary included traveling by van from Srinagar in Kashmir to Ladakh by way of the Himalayas. Seven tourists had signed up, including me. The eighth member of our party was the tour leader, Ramesh Gopandur. Only my fascination with India enabled me to endure traveling in close quarters for three weeks with people I didn't care for. In fairness, the tall podiatrist Tom and his quiet blonde wife Millie were OK. They were intelligent and respectful of Indian culture. And I learned a lot about feet.

A 60-something John Wayne double, who was in fact named John, also was along. He was anything but heroic. John and his sidekick Frank had come to "do" India. They were bored just about everywhere but the Taj Mahal and the duty-free shops at Delhi's airport. Stocky Josie, whose white straw hat was always clean and perfectly balanced on her short black hair, complained about the August heat and the insects.

And Rhoda, tanned and muscled, routinely tossed her olive rucksack onto the best seat in our tour van, an unstuck window that offered air and views and was far from the rear axle's rough ride.

What I resented most about Josie and Rhoda, besides their ignoring me and lack of awe for India, was that they had met Elsie, who was German, at the pre-trip planning meeting I was unable to attend. Sizing her up instantly, they colluded to pawn her off on me. I was only a name tag without a body then, so I understood that their move was an impersonal survival tactic. Thus, Josie and Rhoda became roommates, and I was paired in absentia with Elsie. I silently cursed them for their accurate instincts when I arrived in Delhi from California, jet lagged and headachy, and discovered that Elsie had gotten to the hotel first. In our room she had divided all bathroom objects in half: towels, washcloths, soaps, water glasses, matchbooks, and toilet paper rolls. She had created an invisible Berlin Wall that I was forbidden to cross.

My timing with Elsie was always rotten. I opened the drapes to let in the sun and enjoy a breathtaking view of Delhi from our 16-story hotel just when Elsie wanted to take an afternoon nap. I rattled the pages of my novel just as she decided to retire for the night. I turned on my long-awaited shower just when she wanted to brush her teeth. I ordered a pungent curry just as she concluded she couldn't tolerate the smell of lamb. She chastised me in her clipped German accent when I rumpled the bathmat in our Lake Dal, Kashmir, houseboat.

When I saw her swimming alone late one afternoon in a stagnant pool in whose green water I was about to risk my life, I nearly turned back. But I was hot, dusty and desperate for a dip, so I camouflaged my chagrin with a cheery, "Hi Elsie, how's the water?" "How should I know?" barked Elsie, without a break in her backstroke. Stunned, I slid into the slime. Elsie flutter-kicked furiously to the shallow end of the pool and pointedly climbed out, leaving me alone with the growing swarm of mosquitoes.

That's when I'd had it.

Elsie's relentless provocations could only be blocked if I paid a budget-breaking supplement for a single room. Ramesh was not happy with discord in the ranks, but neither did he want to exert himself to procure extra accommodations along our itinerary. I alternated between helpless supplicant and irate consumer and finally got my room. Elsie benefited from my abdication by not having to pay the extra tariff for solo occupancy. Yet, for the remainder of the voyage, her icy glares were the closest thing to air conditioning in 106-degree heat.

On a sun-filled Kashmiri morning a week into our trip, we were about to depart for Ladakh in our tarnished blue van. My throat was scratchy and my forehead feverish, though I realized these could be symptoms of stress. I asked Ramesh how long the journey to Ladakh would take, wondering if I could handle it.

"Not to worry. It's about nine hours. We go through Zojila Pass and take a rest stop in Kargil. Then on past Lamarayu and down to Leh, the capital of Ladakh. It's a spectacular ride, really."

I believed Ramesh, but for such a long trip it was imperative for me to get a good seat in the van. Bouncing over the rooftop of the world would not improve my health. My luggage and I were at the door of the van uncharacteristically early, before the others showed up. I chose a right-side window seat in the first row behind the driver.

Soon Rhoda climbed into the van, ready to toss her rucksack like a shot-put onto her targeted seat. She was astounded to see me. With a blend of surprise and outrage, she yelped, "Nadine, you're sitting in my seat. That's my seat!"

"I don't see your name on it," I retorted, fed up with being amiable, and added, "It's not written that you get to have the best seat every time we ride."

"You have to give me that seat. Everyone knows I always sit there."

"Not this time. I'm not getting up."

In Rhoda's world of entitlement, it never occurred to her that I might put up a fight. But emboldened by my fever, I didn't budge.

She stomped to a lumpy seat behind me, and I knew that war had been declared. "The enemy of my enemy is my friend," it has been said, and now Elsie, whom Rhoda held in contempt, was to be her ally against me. I pressed my hot forehead against the cool windowpane and vowed to focus on what I came for: the privilege of visiting a remote and sacred region of India. As the other passengers settled themselves into the van, our driver jumped in and started the engine. It coughed, spluttered, then caught, and we lurched west from Srinagar toward the snow-capped Himalayas.

The nine-hour ride turned into 40 hours, during which we ate only one meal. Our van broke down seven times, and we had to hitch a ride in another van while our driver went begging for yet another fan belt. Possibly worst of all were those last hours in the middle of the night when Josie kept singing "It's A Long Way to Tipperary" as we inched our way forward. My sore throat worsened, and when at last we arrived bedraggled in our hotel lobby, I was informed that a single room had not been reserved for me. I would have to bunk with Elsie.

I confess with embarrassment that I had a temper tantrum on the spot. It was directed at Ramesh for his negligence in this important matter. The entire tour group and hotel staff observed me in disapproving silence as I ranted. So dedicated was Elsie to my misfortune that even though she was about to become my fellow victim in Ramesh's room mistake, she smirked triumphantly.

After a long and painful interval during which I was treated like a pariah, I was assigned a single room kept in reserve for visiting Indian VIPs. I regarded the brass key attached to a circular piece of rough wood as a finer treasure than any jewel bestowed by Moghul emperor Shah Jahan on his beloved wife Mumtaz. Once inside my sanctuary, I fell into bed. Before I had time to dream, it was morning.

Because our arrival in Leh had been delayed by a day, and we were scheduled to fly out to Delhi the next morning, Ramesh decided to compress two days of sights into one. So we were on the go from 7 a.m. to 4 p.m., visiting three spectacular Buddhist monasteries, and now we had free time before dinner. I decided to forego a nap and wander into town. Needless to say, no one was interested in joining me. I grabbed my purse, key and camera and started out on the dirt road just outside the hotel. I passed a swimming hole on my right and paused to watch skinny children jump with glee into the dirty water. Their splashes and laughter followed me down the road as it curved to the left, sloped downhill and became the main and only street in the town of Leh.

I walked in fascination past small shops, stalls and clusters of women with brown, wizened faces and rotten teeth. Their strange black stovepipe hats and garments contrasted with the orange, red and yellow produce in front of them. They hadn't sold much but were having a grand time, and their giggles punctured the thin mountain air. I pantomimed a request to photograph them, and their grins indicated delight at this unusual break in their routine.

On my left I noticed a small jewelry shop and made a mental note to stop in after I visited the open-air market at the end of the street. A young man leaning against the doorway observed my glance and beckoned me to come in. His manner was gracious rather than insistent, and I indicated with a smile that I'd come by later.

The market, set against the backdrop of mountains, did not disappoint, and in joyful delirium I shot some more photos. I watched many local families hunting for supplies, from pots to pitchers to prayer wheels and incense. I was told that Leh was a stop on the fabled Silk Road, and soon I was lost in time. Quicker than I wished, the blood-orange sun dropped low in the sky, and I managed a last loving shot of two girls about 6 in bright cotton shirts balancing terra cotta urns on their heads. What the urns contained I didn't know, but I imagined them filled with spices in resplendent pepper reds and saffron yellows.

After a last, lingering look, I returned to the storefronts and easily spotted the jewelry shop. The young man was still at the doorway and appeared to be waiting for me. Appraising him more carefully now, I noted he was handsome: shiny black hair, pale skin, huge brown eyes, high cheekbones and an aquiline nose. Though slender, he had presence, enhanced by his long white *kameez*, the Indian tunic, lightly embroidered with sparkling silver thread. He looked to be in his early-20s.

The shop was dark and narrow with a glass counter at the rear.

As I savored the silver and turquoise rings, the garnet necklaces and multi-color stone jewelry boxes, the young man asked where I was from. I was pleased he hadn't pegged me immediately as an American, though in spite of my own *kameez* I clearly didn't hail from the Indian subcontinent. I said I came from California and wondered if he had grown up in Ladakh.

"I'm from Afghanistan," the stranger announced with pride. My attention swung from the rings to his face, and now the person became more important than the trinkets.

It so happened that my college boyfriend had joined the Peace Corps years back and had been sent to Afghanistan. In those days we thought the assignment was akin to being exiled in Siberia. Somewhere in a box at home I had a collection of two years of airmail letters from Kabul and Kandahar. But that was long ago. I knew well the conflicts that had taken place in the region since then.

"What's your name?" I asked the young man.

"Tarik. What's yours, madam?" I replied and peppered him with questions. "Are you from Kabul? Where did you learn English? How did you get from Afghanistan to India?" And more.

Tarik was patient with my exuberant interrogation.

"Yes, I am from Kabul. I learned English at school. My father was a shopkeeper. I was a child when the Russians invaded. We hated them but tried to go about our lives the best we could. I wanted to be a *mujahid* —I think you must know it means a fighter. My father forbade me to risk my life, and my mother was crying, so out of respect I obeyed them. Life got harder and harder. When I was older, we took what things we could carry and made it to the border near Jalalabad. Then we walked through the mountain passes and finally reached Pakistan. The trip was very difficult."

Tarik brushed a lock of black hair from his furrowed brow.

"We were cold, scared, exhausted. Luckily my father had connections in India. My family lives in Delhi now, and I'm here in Leh because I'm trying to earn money to go to university, and the mountains remind me of home." His eyes began to pool with tears. He blinked them dry and added, "Yes, the mountains, they comfort me."

Tarik talked earnestly, seemingly without guile. I was awed by his family's terrifying escape and impressed with his drive to make a better life. I was thrilled that fate had brought me to a person whose life experience was so different from mine. Tarik was equally curious, and I found myself uncharacteristically at ease revealing things about myself to him.

Here I was — an ex-New Yorker, a reborn Californian, a clinical psychologist, a woman on the down-slope to middle age— chatting cozily with this 20-something stranger. An aura filled his little shop like vapor from a genie's lamp, softening boundaries, blurring nationalities, ethnicities, religions, even gender. We felt like old friends. My best Berkeley chum would have remarked, "Obviously you two knew each other in a past life."

A glance at my watch brought me back to this life and the fact that it was nearly dinner time. I returned to my original purpose: buying souvenirs. I narrowed down Tarik's lovely wares to a ring, a prayer wheel and a tiny reliquary in hues of ivory and amber. I began the customary bargaining, and we settled on a fair price. Tarik wrapped my purchases in plain paper with the care one would expect from Tiffany's and presented the packet to me with a flourish. I shook Tarik's hand, bade him farewell and turned toward the doorway.

"Wait, Miss Nadine, it's time for me to close the shop. Might I be permitted to escort you to your hotel?" Tarik's request was so quaintly put, I found it difficult to resist. A few moments of internal struggle between my paranoid and trusting sides resulted in consent. Tarik turned off the single dim light and locked the door to his shop. We stepped out into the now-empty street. Within two minutes, as we passed the last store, night's curtain descended.

"Why is the electricity off?" I asked nervously. "It's dark everywhere."

"We don't need light anymore," Tarik replied evenly.

His reply was disconcertingly enigmatic, but I didn't challenge it. We both became silent. I wondered if this was a comfortable silence between friends or an uneasy prelude to something sinister. But the stars commanded my attention and drew me from rumination into reverie.

That brush of Tarik's hand against mine, skin on skin, subtle, seductive, brought me back to fear.

I was alone with stars and a stranger.

Tarik remained quiet. I attempted to calm myself with measured breathing. As in a parable, we arrived at a fork in the road. Tarik's voice startled me out of my morbid thoughts.

"Which way to your hotel?"

"To the right."

But everything was changed in the nocturnal world, and I was no longer sure of my direction. We walked farther. Nothing looked familiar.

"What is your hotel's name?" he inquired.

To my shock, I couldn't remember. We'd arrived late the night before and had been out the door early this morning. Then I remembered my key — the hotel name would be on it. I dug into my daypack and with relief pulled out the key. I held it up to Tarik. Heads together and squinting at the wooden tag in the dark, we saw there was no name — not even a room number.

"Can you name all the hotels here?" I asked. "There can't be more than a few, and I may recognize one of them." Tarik claimed ignorance about Leh's hotels. How could this be when he runs a souvenir shop, I thought. Fear was gnawing at my stomach now.

Then I remembered the pond and the children. A marker. I informed Tarik that the pond would be on our left, and it was not far from my hotel. He acted as if a pond near town was news. His continued apparent lack of knowledge about Leh's environs did little to slow my racing heart. We walked on. No pond.

Soon we glimpsed shadows approaching on the road. As they got closer, I saw they were three men — locals. "Let's ask them if they know about hotels," I exclaimed. Tarik tensed; he grabbed my wrist hard.

"Quiet! Don't speak!" he ordered in a harsh whisper. "I'll greet them normally. These types are trouble. They carry knives."

He nodded pleasantly to the men, still holding me firmly, and quickened our pace as we passed. His palm was sweaty, his jaw was clenched.

Then it hit me. Tarik was afraid, too.

In that instant I knew with certainty that he would not harm me. Yet my fear intensified because I knew also with certainty that Tarik was keenly aware of danger from these men. My stranger was my friend after all. But unarmed, and outnumbered, he would not be able to protect me, a vulnerable female guest in his adopted country. Moreover, if something dire were to happen to me, and I never made it back to my hotel, no one in my tour group would search for me, or worry. Well, Ramesh would care about losing face and probably his job, but by then it would be too late.

I was terrified.

We simply had to find my hotel. Forcing ourselves to walk at an even pace so as not to signal fear to the men who were still lumbering down the road, we moved forward. Eventually, through some trees and underbrush off to our right, I spied a yellow glow.

"Tarik, that might be the hotel!"

He responded nervously, "Let's not risk following the curve of the road in that direction. We're safer cutting through these trees."

I let Tarik lead me by the hand, still stunned by his sense of danger, which amplified my own. Striding as fast and as stealthily as we could manage for five long, heart-pounding minutes, we emerged at last into a clearing. There, a few yards ahead, was my hotel's illuminated entrance. Tarik released my hand. We looked into each other's eyes with relief. But was there something more in that intense gaze, something dangerous in a different way? I wasn't sure. A few seconds passed, and we were at the door to the lobby.

In the delicious safety of return, my doubts and self-involvement ebbed. Insight arrived. Of course! Tarik must have lived in fear like this — and worse — throughout the many days and weeks of his family's escape from Afghanistan. Flooded with empathy, I wanted to hug him. So I did. He accepted my affection with neither embarrassment nor greed.

The invitation was now mine.

"Please, Tarik, you must come in and have dinner with me," I urged, impassioned. "My tour group will be in the dining room, but I'm not close with them, and I don't care what they think. I want these Americans to know that people here are more than just exotic sights to be photographed. I want them to know how kind and good you are."

"Thank you, Miss Nadine, but I do not need to meet them. You are the one I am honored to escort."

"I think we share the honor of each other's company, Tarik. All the more reason for you to stay and eat. We can sit at a separate table. It's late. You must be hungry."

"No. I am OK." He moved closer to me with a nearly imperceptible bow. "I must go now. You are a fine lady. I will not forget you. I wish you a safe flight to Delhi, *inshallah*. Please to enjoy your remaining days in India."

With those final words, Tarik kissed me softly on the lips, then slipped into the night. Perhaps because he vanished so quickly, perhaps because I was too shaken to think clearly, perhaps because an old soul part of me knew not to cling, I didn't ask him to change his mind or exchange addresses. His face is no longer as clear in my mind as it once was, but I have not forgotten him. The stars still shine brilliantly over Ladakh, I'm sure, but I shall never know what has become of my noble stranger in exile from his war-torn land.

Nadine Michèle Payn is a writer and retired clinical psychologist. She hosted a popular psychology call-in show in San Francisco in the 1980s, was a contributing editor to the Berkeley Insider magazine, and has written for a number of other publications. She developed a taste for travel at age 15 and loves to write about her many adventures and misadventures around the globe. Her latest daring journey was moving from Berkeley, CA, to Houston, TX, where she lives with her husband and two cats.

THAILAND'S LOST CHILDREN
Thailand

It's almost 9 p.m. and Chiang Rai's Night Bazaar is still swarming with people. A group of young girls performs a traditional Thai dance in the market square, their lithe arms swirling in graceful chorus. Most locals don't bother to watch, too busy with friends and catching up on the weekly gossip.

Dozens of vendors line the walkways, hawking products from iron cookware to traditional Thai clothing. They raise hopeful eyes to my daughter Kirstin and me as we worm our way through the market's narrow aisles. The melodic tones of the Thai language are an unintelligible, yet soothing, buzz in my ears and, for a moment, the English thoughts running through my head seem foreign.

Ten-year-old Kirstin doesn't seem to notice the new-ness, the strangeness of it all. She giggles with excitement, holding tight to my hand while she marches ahead, as if in search of some great treasure.

Here, in this tiny square of Northern Thailand, our lives in Colorado seem distant, opaque. In the warm night air, I sense something I can't quite identify. A slower pace of life, perhaps? A feeling of safety? What-ever it is, I am starting to relax, intrigued with the world around me.

I can nearly forget that this is not just a simple vaca-tion and ignore the fact that I have come here to write about the sex trade.

"Come on!" Kirstin says, pulling me toward the rich smell of spicy food,

The colorful dishes, neatly displayed, all look so ap-petizing, except for the plates of grilled crickets, beetles and grasshoppers.

"Wanna try some, mom?" my daughter asks, a mis-chievous tone in her voice.

"Maybe later," I say. "Right now, I can't stand the thought of eating bug legs."

There are limits, after all, to one's adventurous spirit.

Kirstin and I are obviously outsiders, the only blondes in the market. But the Thai are kind and wel-coming, and Kirstin mirrors their pleasant grins. We stop at a jewelry stand where I look over several gold neck-laces.

"It's so cheap," Kirstin exclaims, after asking the prices.

The American dollar is strong here, making our purchases quite affordable. And while all economic strata are found in Thailand, the majority of people live comfortable, simple lives.

While I pore over the necklaces, the middle-age saleswoman smiles and admires Kirstin's golden locks. We don't understand her words, but the stroking of the hair and friendly pat on the head is universal. A complimentary child's bracelet is tossed in on top of our purchase. Kirstin hugs it to her body as we walk away.

"The Thai seem to like children," I remark to my friend Nancy, who joins us later at the market.

"Of course," she replies. "The Thai love their children and the children of others as well; kids are something to be treasured here."

I nod my head, deferring to Nancy's wisdom. She has lived in Thailand for several years, raising two sons with her husband.

Still, I am confused. Her take on Thailand's purported adoration of children seems at odds with its thriving child prostitution. I open my mouth to ask about this paradox, but Nancy turns down another aisle.

When I reach her, she is speaking with four young women resting on a blanket, their handicrafts in neat rows in front of them. They wear dresses covered in intricate beadwork; vibrant headdresses adorned with coins and beads sit atop their heads. Shy smiles reveal red gums and teeth from chewing betel nut leaves, a popular habit.

The women speak to each other and Nancy in clipped sounds foreign to my ears, quite different from the Thai language.

"They are Akha," Nancy says.

Instantly, I'm intrigued.

The Akha are one of six distinct tribes living in the nearby hills of Northern Thailand. Each of the hill tribes has its own language and culture. Considered outsiders in their own country, the tribes lead remote, primitive lives. Village homes are often made of bamboo and thatched roofs, most without electricity or running water.

Rejected by the Thai, many of the 540,000 tribal people do not possess Thai citizenship, as documenting births in grass huts far from modern hospitals is difficult. Lack of official status denies the villages fundamental rights, like education, voting and land ownership.

As an agrarian society, the inability to own land is problematic for the tribes. As soil is depleted, tribes migrate between the steep hills of Thailand and neighboring countries. Recent government mandates force those who stay in Thailand to cultivate the same plot of land over and over, a distinct change from former ways.

The pressures of modernization have intensified hardships for the Akha, making the villagers more susceptible to the social ills of civilized cultures. The least-educated and poorest of the hill tribes, the Akha maintain the highest rate of drug addiction and infant mortality in Thailand. Opium addiction and, sadly, child prostitution are huge issues for the tribe.

*****

I'm here to write an article on child prostitution for a Chicago newspaper. It's a problem that has plagued many nations, but in Thailand it has reached endemic proportions.

I'm hoping that more media exposure about the consequences of prostitution will shrink the allure of this social blight. Personally, I'm searching for a glimmer of hope, a fine shimmer of light that illuminates the goodness of humanity.

But that won't be easy to find. Young children are prized commodities in the sex tourism trade in Thailand. Despite the government's efforts — it's spent millions of dollars on programs and law enforcement — relief agencies estimate that there are more than two million prostitutes in Thailand, 800,000 of them under age 16.

Glancing at my daughter, her face shining with innocence, I am sickened. What kind of person willingly takes that away from a child? An intense feeling of protectiveness overwhelms me; I want to keep all the evils of the world from my child. So, once again, I question.

Was I wise to bring Kirstin along on this trip? Child prostitution is a provocative subject for an adult, and even more so for a 10-year-old girl. Though I knew the trip would be challenging, I selfishly wanted Kirstin with me as our busy lives — school, sports, work — leave little opportunity for one-on-one time with my kids. Thailand, I had been told, was a safe and wonderful place.

"Why not bring one of your kids along?" Nancy had suggested.

Although Kirstin won't be privy to the interviews, she knows the topic I'm here to research. We've had simple conversations, at her age level, about what we might see, but Kirstin is still struggling to understand.

"How can they stand to do that, mom?" she asks when I try to explain the sex trade.

I have no answer.

I have the same questions myself.

How do I explain that there are parents or aunties and uncles who willingly sell their children into sex slavery? That other children, with no parents or means of support, take to the streets to fill their empty stomachs? That others prostitute themselves for drug money or to fuel a lavish lifestyle?

Rooted in poverty and primal human behavior, child prostitution seems an insurmountable problem. How can it be addressed?

I pose this question to Nancy, who thinks a moment before answering.

"By helping one life at a time," she says.

Nancy has spent the last 10 years doing just that. Originally an interpreter for the deaf, she spent several years working on Christian social welfare projects before moving to Thailand. There she met her husband, an Akha pastor. Although it was hard to leave America, she knew her new life was in Thailand, where she and her husband now run a children's home and work with the Hill Tribe people.

Finished with our purchases, Nancy directs Kirstin and me down a dark side street. Such places in the States are not always safe, so my senses are heightened to danger.

"Is this OK?" I ask, referring to the dark alleys and the red lights of the Go-Go bars up ahead.

Three young men walk in the shadows behind us. I can't help but wonder if they plan to do us harm. Nancy assures me that we are safe. She stops in front of a bar, and I turn to see what she sees.

Young girls, some in their early teens, others approaching 20, congregate outside the bars. Dressed in jeans and T-shirts, a few wearing short skirts, they look like average teenagers.

"They're prostitutes," Nancy says, a sad note in her voice.

The announcement shocks me. The girls don't look anything like the prostitutes I've seen in American movies.

But the girls are rooted to their spots in front of the bars, a dead giveaway, Nancy says. We walk farther, passing dozens of young girls — and boys — who make this their profession.

As we walk past one bar, the girls out front notice Nancy's Akha bag with its recognizable stitching. It's a slow night, so they call out "hello" in Akha. They are shocked when Nancy responds in their native tongue, since very few people can speak the Akha language.

Three prostitutes, the youngest possibly 13, the oldest about 19, admire Nancy's bag and then turn their attention to Kirstin.

One strokes Kirstin's locks, the other drapes an arm around her and looks into her large blue eyes. Kirstin can't understand their words and, at first, she pulls away in fright. But Nancy shows only kindness and compassion. She continues to exchange pleasantries with the teens. My daughter picks up on Nancy's calm manner and grins shyly back at the girls.

Nancy tells them that we are visiting from America. They smile. Why are we here? Do we like it? Does Kirstin like her straight blonde hair?

We end up taking pictures of the girls with Kirstin, posed and smiling in the middle. The girls smile too, perhaps sadly, and I wonder if they sense that our meeting has made my heart heavy. I wonder about the dreams each has given up.

Eventually, it's time to move on. We wave goodbye and continue down the sidewalk, past foreign men who seem to have local "girlfriends." Kirstin clings to my hand in silence. There is a somber look in her eyes. She seems to have sensed the gravity of what we're seeing;

still, I don't think she truly grasps all that has transpired here tonight.

"Why don't they just go home?" she asks of the girls we spoke to. "Why don't they stop it, if they don't like it?"

I try to explain that some may not have good homes to go home to; that maybe this is the only way they think they can earn a living.

A look of shocked realization crosses Kirstin's face. It is, perhaps, the first time she has considered what she has — a family, a home.

I'm struck by the strange dichotomy of Thailand: In a country where child prostitution is a huge problem, those children born into stable homes are loved and well-provided for, but those who are born into poverty or to drug-addicted parents face a different fate. The lure of wealth from prostitution is strong, even if it is a child who is forced to be the bread earner.

That night, I dream of the girls with sad faces.

*****

The next morning dawns bright, a perfect day for heading upriver to the Karen tribal village of Ruammit. We plan to explore the village and pursue one of Kirstin's dreams — riding an elephant. We hire a boat and driver in Ban Thatorn. Nancy is our guide for the day, and she brings her two boys along.

The long, slim craft doesn't look very steady, but we're soon skimming up the Mae Kok. Within minutes, the city is behind us. Tall mountains covered with green trees and thick grasses rise from the river banks. No people or animals are in sight, except for one lone hawk circling overhead.

Eventually, the hills grow larger and I see my first tribal village high on the mountainside. The huts, most of them on bamboo stilts, look like little wooden dots in the emerald-forested land.

A few minutes later, Kirstin sits up and points with excitement. Following her finger, I see several elephants in the river, playing in the water. At least 10 of them huddle together near the bank, paying no mind to us.

Two men struggling to hold onto a 15-foot boa constrictor greet us as we scramble ashore. Smiling, they ask if I'd like to have my picture taken with the snake draped around me. I glance at the massive creature writhing about on their shoulders, and shake my head no. Kirstin walks far around the big snake.

Behind the men, several elephants walk around freely. It's unnerving when they reach out their massive trunks, looking for a handout. One animal reaches its trunk to Kirstin, who shrieks and grabs my hand.

Nancy, who has clearly been here dozens of times, pushes the elephants' trunks away and makes her way past them. Kirstin clings to my hand as we follow cautiously behind, while one of Nancy's sons rushes to buy a bunch of bananas to feed the beasts. This is a treat for the boys, who are happy and at ease here.

Nancy speaks to the Karen villagers in Thai, who also speak this as their second language. "It's 150 baht for an elephant ride," she says. "Give it a try!"

Kirstin takes a determined breath and walks over to the elephants. We purchase a ride from the villagers, and then mount rickety stairs to a high wooden platform. Gingerly, we crawl onto a rough chair that has been tied to the elephant's back. The handler hops on the creature's head, and we're off.

Not prepared for the creature's jilted footsteps, I support myself with both arms to keep from being thrown into Kirstin. She giggles.

"This is hard, mom!" she exclaims. "It's kind of bouncy!"

As we make our way down the narrow lanes of the Karen village, chickens dart in front of us, and dogs run about. Occasionally, the elephant handler stops to talk with an acquaintance; at other times the elephant halts to pull at a grassy snack. Nothing hurries here.

I can see into several of the stilted huts, where women are cooking or stitching. Kirstin looks as well. Does she notice there are no lights or toilets? How different this must seem from our home in Colorado. Do the straw walls and dirt floors shock her? My daughter says nothing, but I can see she is deep in thought.

Settled in the foothills, the Karen tribes depend on farming and hunting for game. The women dress in colorful blouse-sarong combinations, their long hair often pulled back in buns or covered with white scarves.

My body is stiff after the elephant ride, but the soreness is forgotten when we stop at a local village store-restaurant. Aside from the rice, I have never seen most of the food we are served. A tad spicy and quite delicious, at $2 a plate it's a bargain. Kirstin and I smile at each other over our plates of food.

"Wasn't that cool?" she asks, still thinking about the elephant ride.

Perhaps this will be one of those memories that will linger in the back of her mind, resurfacing years later when she has children of her own. I'm grateful to be a part of that memory; to have this precious time with my oldest daughter.

We walk around the dirt roads, looking at shops and talking with villagers. Many of the homes seem empty; others have a chair here, a table there. Kirstin's eyes are wide as she soaks in the scenes. This is her first glance at the unrelenting grip of poverty. She is quiet as we head back to the river bank, where our driver is waiting.

The ride back to town is chilly, and I'm glad I have a jacket. Kirstin snuggles close for warmth, and within minutes is sound asleep. Nancy's boys are fast asleep too. Smiling at each other, Nancy and I pull our children close. My mind plays back the scene in the village. I wonder what it is like to raise children there.

Is it harder to raise children when you don't have all the comforts that materialistic goods can offer? Or it is simpler without the distractions of having to provide stylish clothing, constant entertainment and a lovely home? A child's happiness does not come from things bought with cash, but from the love and support of a caring family. Perhaps, like mothers everywhere, Akha women simply try to make the best possible life for their children; meeting their basic needs, protecting them from harm, and loving them as only parents can. Aren't these common bonds of motherhood, whether lived out in a stately mansion or a simple hut, universal?

*****

Later that week, Nancy takes us to the children's home that she and her husband have started. When our car approaches, we see dozens of girls outside playing basketball. Nearly 80 tribal girls live at the home, ranging in age from 7 to 23. All of them attend Thai school and take courses in English and their native Akha. They are dressed in worn, but neat, clothing. I can hear laughter and quick chatter.

"They built that court themselves," Nancy says, pointing out the large, slightly uneven concrete court. "We told them we could only pay for the materials, so they put in the concrete themselves."

A group of girls comes to greet Nancy, their faces beaming. They hug her when she gets out of the car. Kirstin looks at the girls through the car window. The girls stare back.

The children have come to the home under varying circumstances. Some were rescued, like the 8-year-old whose father tried to sell her into prostitution to support his opium addiction; others have lost both parents to AIDS and were at risk of being sold to the sex trade by relatives.

"And that girl," Nancy says, pointing to a 12-year-old, "came to us when the house was full. Her uncle brought her in because her parents had died of AIDS, and said he didn't want the girl. She was hiding behind him, crying. I just melted and I took her anyway."

Nancy turns her attention to the group of girls, speaking in words I can't understand.

"These are our girls," she says, with obvious affection and pride.

"Nice to meet you," one 10-year-old says meekly, holding out her hand to me.

The girls immediately surround Kirstin, giggling and covering their mouths with their hands.

Kirstin tosses me a questioning look.

"They like your hair," Nancy says.

One of the girls bravely reaches out her hand to stroke Kirstin's hair and soon there are more tiny brown arms stroking her head. I search for concern on my daughter's face, but she senses the girls' kindness, and laughs.

Another girl motions for Kirstin to come play basketball with them. "Can I go with them, mom?" she asks.

"Of course," I say, shooing her off to play.

Nancy and I walk into one of the simple eating rooms of the house. There are no screens on the wide open windows, the chilly night air wafting in. The home has no heat or hot water, so I keep my coat on like everyone else in the room.

From my perch near the window, I can see Kirstin and the girls at play.

There are happy shouts, and playful teases coming from the court. A peaceful feeling permeates this home, a contrast from the streets.

The door opens abruptly and several younger girls spill into the room. Kirstin is in the center, hair now in two neat braids.

"Molleigh did my hair for me," she says, nodding to the girl beside her.

"And look what Molleigh made me," she adds, holding up some beautiful needlework.

"Can we come back here tomorrow?" my daughter asks.

I nod, and she heads back outside with the girls.

Through the window, my eyes follow these girls who will soon become women, hopeful futures spreading out before them. Kirstin's arm is linked in Molleigh's. Several other girls skip alongside them. Language barriers and economic and cultural differences don't seem to matter; tonight Kirstin has found a kindred spirit.

I'm grateful that I've brought my daughter to Thailand. For it is here that she has begun to grasp truths that some take a lifetime to learn.

Tomorrow there will be more girls to interview, more heartache to see. But tonight, in a place where money is scarce but love abundant, I have seen the smiles of contented lives.

As the moon rises into the cloudless sky, I hear more giggles. The girls, most with straight shiny black hair and one with locks the color of honey, are playing basketball again. I look at Kirstin, whose petite frame has seemed to grow on this trip, and wonder if she knows how proud of her I am.

A breeze sweeps through the window and into the room. I catch the smell of wild Poinsettias. I stop for a moment and make a mental memory. It is a beautiful night to be in Thailand.

Janna Graber is a Colorado-based journalist, editor and producer who has written for more than 40 publications. She has a special love for travel journalism, and is the managing editor at Go World Travel Magazine (GoWorldTravel.com). She is the editor of two travel anthology books: Chance Encounters: Travel Tales from Around the World (World Traveler Press) and Adventures of a Lifetime (World Traveler Press). Follow her @AColoradoGirl or see jannagraber.com.

TRAVEL CHARADES
Around the World

There is an old joke that now seems to personify globalization. It's the one that asks "What do you call someone who speaks three languages? Trilingual. What do you call someone who speaks two languages? Bilingual. What do you call someone who speaks one language? American."

I think this joke needs a postscript: "What would you call someone who speaks one language universally?"

My answer is not "Esperanto linguist," but rather a "Travel Charadist"— someone who speaks Travel Charades. It works as a universal language and has worked wonderfully well for a woman alone in the world.

With Travel Charades I've adapted the old parlor game where you act out meanings without using words. I lapse into this mode of conversation in places I visit where I don't speak the native language. That would be almost everywhere that French is not the native language.

Travel Charades is remarkably useful in asking a question or conveying an idea, a concept or an expression — something basic — by acting it out. And, surprisingly, I've almost always received a helpful answer from a knowledgeable native.

Of course, it would be infinitely preferable to try and learn the local language, even becoming fluent. But the world is so full of interesting places that I don't want to restrict myself to countries where the population either speaks dependable English or tolerates rusty, poorly accented French. I'd rather grab the suitcase and go with Travel Charades as my fallback language system.

Certainly, it doesn't allow for meaningful dialogues about such things as comparative philosophies or political theory. But, then, such subjects are ill-suited for casual acquaintanceship anyway.

Travel Charades saved me when I ran out of hairspray in St. Petersburg, Russia. This is not a United Nations level problem, I know. But somewhere between an exhaustive tour of the vast treasures of the Hermitage and a bedazzling day amid the splendors of the Czars' palaces, I discovered the need to replenish my supply of hair elixir, brand unimportant. Nevsky Prospect, in the heart of St. Petersburg's tourist district, was a short walk from our hotel and, I assumed, an obvious place to find a commodity sought by female tourists.

Without a group or tour guide to run interference, and with my Russian limited to the pleasantries of "good morning" and "thank you," I entered a brightly lit shop crowded with pharmacy items, all sporting Russian labels. Four cheerful young salesgirls in stiff white pharmacy smocks clustered by a counter and I asked if anyone spoke English. They shook their heads in unison: "nyet."

Using cross-cultural girl-to-girl language, however, I made my request. First I cocked my hand by my head as if I were depressing the nozzle of a container of hair spray and pretended to spray my hair while making the appropriate sound. "Fffttt, fffttt," I said. "Fffttt, fffttt." They smiled and led me to the hair products shelf.

I inspected the assorted products and pointlessly read the labels for clues. So I resumed my Travel Charades dialogue. Then I pretended to squirt something on my hands and rub it into my hair —washing — and shook my head "no." I mimicked blow-drying my hair, making a "bzzz, bzzz" sound, again shaking my head "no." I evoked the motions of using a curling iron and brushing the hair in place, shaking my head "no" for each. And then I repeated the charade of spraying my newly coiffed hair in place, uttered a couple of more "fffttts" and smilingly shook my head "yes."

The cheerful salesgirls twittered and conferred among themselves, then ceremoniously selected a silver plastic vial with a royal blue cap, which they shyly presented. I removed the cap, revealing the miracle of an aerosol sprayer of hair fixative. I grinned broadly, they grinned in return; I bowed, they bowed; I paid the specified number of rubles on the tag, and left exhausted, but with hair spray to fight the Russian humidity and a renewed belief in the power of my universal language.

Travel Charades was equally useful when I got lost wandering around Kala, the old section of Tbilisi, in the Republic of Georgia. While on a week-long business trip to the former Soviet republic, I had one independent morning in Tbilisi so I determined to strike out to see the historic quarter. First, I stopped at Prospero's Bookstore on Rustaveli Street in the most cosmopolitan and well-touristed part of town and bought a tourist map, which carefully delineated each of the quarter's narrow, winding streets with a readable, anglicized name. "Leselidze Str," for example.

With map in hand, I headed for the area and meandered through the narrow lanes, delighting in intricately carved wooden balconies, layers of architecture that climbed higgledy-piggledy up the hill toward the looming silver statue of Mother of Georgia. I wandered past 19th century buildings, dusty and paint-peeling with stories to tell, and wound my way from one tiny street to another, submersed in Tbilisi's antiquity, until I was totally immersed — and lost. And when I conferred with my map, it was worthless because it was printed with transliterated Georgian; every street sign, however, was etched in beautiful, calligraphic, undecipherable Georgian script. My knowledge of spoken Georgian was —

once again — limited to the token words for "hello" and "thank you." My fallback? Travel Charades.

A bent and elderly woman, draped in black, was making her way home carrying a sack of groceries. Rhetorically, I asked if she spoke English. She shook her head "no." Then I smiled, shrugged my shoulders, and pointed to the nearest street sign — quite undecipherable — and then to my map. I covered my face in a quizzical expression and danced my finger over the part of the map where I thought I might be. She squinted at the map, then shook her head, pointed delicately to one of its tiny lines and waved toward the street sign. I was "there." She turned the map around to orient me.

Now able to strike out in the right direction, I smiled, bowed and murmured "*gmadlobt*" (thank you) and continued threading the labyrinth of old Kala. Twice again, I stopped approachable-looking Tbilisians to re-enact the Travel Charade, to correct or affirm my location. Soon I emerged at Tavisupleba Square, at the foot of familiar Rustaveli Street.

How did you find your way around?" asked my English-speaking host with some amazement when I related my adventure. But I merely grinned and shrugged. In Travel Charades language, it meant that I didn't think he would have understood.

Travel Charades has rescued me in a variety of other situations — changing a car tire in a remote, untouristed part of Turkey; seeking a tiny local market in Andean Ecuador; identifying the correct subway in Santiago. I also got directions (more or less) from a beggar in the Danube town of Arbanasi, Bulgaria, when I lost my way and couldn't remember how to return to my Viking longboat.

Although I've expanded the language as I've traveled, a few gestures remain universal. A shrug, with arms bent, hands extended, and shoulders uplifted, always and unfailingly means "I don't know," which can follow a question or act as an opening gambit. An exaggerated expression of puzzlement translates as "I don't understand — please help me;" and a wide smile followed by a quick bow means "thank you so much."

Today, in a globalized world, we expect English to be everyone else's second language. Or we can whip out a digital language translator app and attempt to pronounce something like the original question or statement. Asking where the bus stop is in Bratislava yields, "*Kde je autobusová zastávka?*" which I couldn't begin to pronounce. Instead, I could show the question to a native on the street or a clerk in a shop to get the answer, but if it came in Slovakian, I'd still be at a loss.

No, I prefer to depend on Travel Charades, although I expect one day to be brought up short by a resident in a host country who also speaks Travel Charades. He or she will place hands on hips and shake his head with a disgusted expression. I can read that. The message will be "Ugh, typical American tourist! Why can't she learn our language?"

He will be entirely right, of course, and I will be chastised. But, as fond as I am of traveling the world, I hope I don't encounter him anytime soon.

Louisiana native Mary Ann Sternberg has lived along the Mississippi River most of her life. She has been a freelance writer and nonfiction author for 40 years, with a specialty in Louisiana culture and history. She also has penned travel and natural history pieces, and personal essays for general interest publications — riding in the Goodyear blimp, adventuring along the Amazon River in Peru and teaching feature writing in the Republic of Georgia, among others. Her bylines have appeared most recently in newyorker.com, Preservation Magazine, The Forward and Louisiana Cultural Vistas. Nonfiction books published by the Louisiana State University Press include Along the River Road (in its third edition), Winding Through Time and River Road Rambler. She is a member of the American Society of Journalists and Authors and the Authors Guild, and works part-time at the LSU School of Mass Communication.

LOVE, LOSS AND LETTING GO ON THE ROAD
Spain

When I travel, I never pack anything of great value. If it wouldn't look right at home in the aisles of Target — or, if I'm honest, on a collapsible card table at a garage sale — it's probably not going in my bag. Even the bag itself is just a battered old suitcase held together with duct tape and hope. After all, who's going to steal that off the luggage carousel?

But there is one very precious item I've taken with me everywhere for years — a delicate sliver of a silver charm. I've no idea what it cost, but it was worth more to me than almost anything else I've ever owned.

On one side, it bears my name. "Amy," that is. "Laughinghouse," as you might imagine, would be bit unwieldy. The other side is embossed with three hieroglyphics that supposedly signify my name's meaning, but which I suspect were actually chosen because they resemble the letters themselves. It's elegant, unusual and, most importantly to me, a gift from my sister Kimberly.

She passed away in 2009, but wearing that pendant, hooked around my neck on a slender chain, I felt that Kim was there, seeing the world with me. I could imagine her wicked cackle of a laugh, the expressive arc of her eyebrows, which communicated her thoughts like semaphores, and the hilarious stories that she could have woven from even the most commonplace event.

So when I happened to notice the chain dangling, unhooked and bereft of this tiny treasure while on a jaunt around the tangled maze of Barcelona's Barri Gotic quarter last autumn, I felt the weight of a loss much greater than the actual mass of that feather-light talisman.

We didn't travel much as kids. Back then, flights were too expensive for a middle-class family of four. Our mom and dad were only able to take us as far as four wheels could carry us. That meant long drives to the beach and yearly jaunts to visit my grandparents 14 hours away, sometimes with three highly vocal Siamese cats in tow.

Their yowling, however, was nothing compared to the arguments that erupted from the back seat. "Kim's on MY side of the car!" "Amy's touching me!" How my father resisted the urge to direct our powder blue station wagon right over the side of a cliff, I'll never know, although it probably had a lot to do with the geographical dearth of cliffs on America's Eastern seaboard.

I think it was the necessarily limited scope of our adventures that birthed the travel bug in both my sister and me. We knew there was a big world beyond Panama City (Florida, that is), and we wanted to see it.

Kim only had the opportunity to travel overseas once — to Paris, doggedly hauling my infant niece in a baby carriage up and down the stairs of Metro stations. But she and her husband, along with my niece and nephew, logged thousands of miles crisscrossing U.S. highways. They thought nothing of driving 12 hours each way for a weekend at Mardi Gras, and they once rented an RV to explore the wilds of Alaska. Our last trip together as a family was to the Big Island of Hawaii for Christmas — which also happened to be my sister's birthday.

Every time I fastened that oblong ornament around my neck, I knew there was some risk I might lose it. But what was the alternative? To leave it lying in a box like a lonely relic? No. I think Kim would have loved to go many of the places I've been fortunate enough to visit (though she might have raised those dark eyebrows at a few), and I was determined to bring her with me however I could.

I wandered the streets of Barcelona that afternoon, eyes glued to the pavement, my heart leaping at the sight of every silver gum wrapper. Still, I knew it would be a miracle if I found the charm.

I didn't. But that doesn't mean there might not be a happy ending to this story after all.

Maybe that adventurous part of Kim's spirit, which the pendant symbolized in my mind, was as inexorably attracted by the warmth and energy of Barcelona as I am. Maybe, as I stood in some lively old square, where laughter and chatter wafted from the buzzing cafes, she slipped quietly away, dropping her kid sister's hand to explore for a while on her own.

I imagine that charm glinting in the blazing sunshine on an old cobblestone steeped in history and trodden by centuries of footsteps, soaking up the heat and the atmosphere. Someone, I'm certain, will notice it eventually. They'll pick it up, and I hope they will wear it, too, as they wander around faraway cities, clamber up mountainsides and whiz over oceans.

I've accepted that I'll never hold it again. But just as my sister sometimes comes back to me in my dreams, so, too, has a form of this memento.

The Christmas after I lost the pendant, on what would have been Kim's 47th birthday, I opened a small white box from my mother. There, glinting on a bed of snowy cotton, was an almost identical pendant. This one is perhaps doubly precious, because it was a gift from my sister to our mother, engraved with my mother's name — and she was entrusting it to me.

As the next chapter of my travels begins, I'll wear this necklace now for both of them.

Am I afraid I might lose it? Absolutely. But at least if I do, I've realized that I don't need a symbol over my heart to carry the people I cherish with me, wherever I go.

London-based travel writer Amy Laughinghouse has attempted to overcome her fears (and sometimes, basic common sense) through her adventures in 30 countries around the world. From paragliding in the Swiss Alps to walking with lions in Mauritius, she dishes on the perks and perils of globetrotting for publications such as Qantas Airlines' magazine, LonelyPlanet.com, GoWorldTravel.com, the Toronto Globe and Mail, and the Dallas Morning News. Her travel tales can also be found on her website, amylaughinghouse.com.

OUR LIFE AFLOAT
South Pacific

Without warning, our boat made a sharp turn. Instead of riding down the 8-foot swells with the wind propelling us from behind, we were now pointing into the waves with the wind coming from ahead. It was as if we'd been skiing down a bunny hill and a rookie mistake caused us to face uphill and slide backward. I jumped into action.

Our ham radio, which allowed us contact with the world beyond our 40-foot catamaran Ceilydh, also created electronic interference and disrupted our autopilot, causing wild 90-degree turns. Over the radio, my husband Evan continued reading out the weather report and recording the locations and conditions aboard the dozen other boats also sailing the 2,800 miles from Puerto Vallarta, Mexico, to the Marquesas, French Polynesia, while I began steering us back on course.

We'd been at sea for 16 days straight, and much of the morning's radio call was spent talking about where we'd make landfall in 48 hours. Evan and our buddy boats, a small group of boat crews with and without kids that we'd befriended in Mexico and planned to sail the South Pacific in loose company with, traded tasteless cannibal jokes and debated the pros and cons of one island port over another (frangipani-scented jungle and towering fairytale mountain peaks versus tropical beaches and exotic villages), while I spun the wheel and adjusted the sails. With growing confusion I realized no matter what I did, the boat remained facing into the liquid hills, shuddering with each wave impact, while the sails flapped uselessly.

"Something's wrong with our steering," I called to Evan. He came to the cockpit and repeated my efforts and then joined me at the back of our boat. Our rudders, which control the steering, are found on each hull's stern.

"I can see this rudder," Evan said as he peered with me into the hypnotic blue depths, seeking out the rectangular shape, "but on the other side there must be an optical illusion, because I can't see that one."

"We can't see it because it isn't there," I said.

"Of course it's there," said Evan, who had now leaned so far over the stern that the frothy sea licked at his hair. Worried he'd be swallowed by one of the bigger waves, I called out our 9-year-old daughter, Maia, for the tie-breaking decision.

"Definitely gone," she said after taking a long look over the side.

Shock was quickly replaced by action. By adjusting the sails and turning on the motor you can steer a catamaran with one rudder. But it's a bit like a car with one-wheel drive; if the course is straight and flat, it's easy. While I reported our predicament to the other boats over the radio, Evan began balancing our boat so one rudder could do the job of two. Cautiously we got back underway. I reassured Maia that losing a rudder was a manageable problem, and then to prove it I gave her some school work; French lessons and the geography of volcanoes to prepare her for landfall.

Outwardly calm, Evan and I looked over the charts to pick the best harbor for our crippled boat (a town with skilled welders beat out tropical beaches and exotic villages) and sent out emails to alert the French Polynesian Coast Guard and ask advice. The sea wasn't flat and our course wasn't straight; waves knocked our boat sideways and my heart lurched in fear. There was a high risk that our remaining rudder could be over powered by a large wave and break off. Having one-wheel was stressful; but no-wheels, hundreds of miles from shore, could lead to abandoning our boat.

*****

Evan and I met as teenagers at sailing instructor school in Vancouver, British Columbia. His plan was to design sailboats while sailing around the world; mine was to write about boats while sailing around the world. We made a good team. Within a few years we married and bought a sturdy little blue-and-white sailboat with round portholes and a swooping bowsprit. Little Ceilydh looked like a traditional seagoing sailboat; and as her 20-something-year-old crew, we were the archetype of young adventurers.

It sounds idyllic, like an endless vacation, and in truth sailing is a wonderfully ancient and meandering way to travel the world. We'd slip into a new port at dawn and watch as the land slowly revealed itself. Practicing our Spanish, we'd be led to the market by giggling children, then haggle over tomatoes with a shy woman who'd ask what snow felt like. In the evenings we'd sit at rickety tables, sharing bottles of tequila and our world views with people from every continent. With the idealism of youth, we were trying to sail toward a more deliberate life — one that just happened to include a few risks.

As a crew of two it was easy to choose adventure over caution. We surprised the locals when we arrived in a small village in El Salvador where we were told we were the first cruising boat after the end of their civil war. Missing men, mortar-pocked buildings and an overflowing prison contrasted with charismatic women who were determined to entice us to try the full range of local cuisine.

It wasn't the threat of *sopa de pata* (tripe soup) or *gallo en chicha* (rooster in a fermented sauce) that saw us leave El Salvador and unwisely sail into a gale. Instead, we left because we wanted to try surfing in Costa Rica. Our first night at sea, when I was on watch and our little boat was being whacked about like a mouse in the clutches of a cat, Evan woke up when our pressure cooker and assorted cutlery were launched across the boat and smashed into the wall beside his head. All this for surfing, something we never really got good at.

Mostly, danger was a story dramatized for other sailors over drinks and then toned down for our parents during our occasional calls home. Our parents shared what friends at home were accomplishing while we were off sailing 12,000 miles to 10 countries: settling into careers, buying houses and having children. But of course, what we were doing also sounded very nice, they said with uncertainty.

We opted to start a family in our own time. Maia was born a couple of years later in an East Coast port thousands of miles from home. A year later we did what everyone expected and sold little Ceilydh and headed home to Canada. Then we got good jobs and bought a home and adopted a little kitten called Charlie. But a few years later we did the unexpected; we all, including Charlie the Cat, moved aboard a bigger Ceilydh and prepared to set off to see the world.

"Why are you taking Maia? Pirates are so dangerous — can't you leave her and Charlie here?" The question from a friend's sister was a familiar one. The implication was sailing as a young couple was an adventure, but sailing as a family was reckless.

We'd met several cruising families while out sailing and at the time it struck us as the perfect way to raise our future child — she'd have ready access to her parents and the world would be both her playground and school. She'd even have her playmate along — a cautious black cat (considered good luck to seafarers) who knew not to venture out of the cabin in bad weather and who quickly developed a preference for tuna over reef fish. But each time I tried to describe the wonders of sailing as a family it sounded irresponsible compared to their more practical concerns about pirates, illness, storms and home-schooling.

Sometimes I tried to explain how we'd thought it through; we'd weighed each risk and prepared for every eventuality. Even still it's a delicate balance to set sail with a child: Would our daughter be safe? Stay healthy? Could we replace her teachers and find her friends? And, yet, we also were looking toward a horizon of unparalleled opportunity: raising a kid for whom the extraordinary becomes ordinary. Swimming with giant manta rays, international celebrations, friends from every continent — this could be the stuff of her childhood.

"She likes whales and being with us. And we'll avoid the regions with pirates," I awkwardly responded.

Each day, each experience, proved sailing was the best way for our family to live. One day as we sailed toward an anchorage in Baja, CA, I saw signs of a whale spouting on the horizon. As we sailed toward it, I called Maia on deck. We saw more spray rising several feet in the air and then started seeing lumpy brown log-like shapes haphazardly drifting on the surface, each one sighing a fine, fetid mist above the placid waves. Taking in the bulbous heads and wrinkled skin, I puzzled over the species, then realized they were sperm whales.

While I did the identification, Maia was counting. "Forty! But that really big log might be two whales so maybe 41!" she called out as we made our way through the super pod, changing course every time another leviathan swam lazily into our path. I tried to tell Maia the story of how the sperm whales had been hunted to near extinction for their oil, grasping, as they floated beside us, how easy slaughtering them must have been. I wanted Maia to know the wonder of seeing a species come back from the brink of destruction. She missed the impromptu home-schooling lesson though, hypnotized by trying to stare down a whale's massive liquid eye.

As we sailed away from the pod, rank whale breath still clinging to our sails, I wondered if I should have tried harder to get her to understand. Then I realized that maybe simply having to tack and change course over and over, just to work our way through an ocean thick with whales was enough.

But on our voyage to the South Pacific on that first rudderless night, when the sun had set but the moon hadn't risen, when I was entering my 14th hour of trying to hide the kind of fear that constricts your breath and coats your skin like a bruise, sailing stopped feeling like a good way for our family to live. Maia was in bed and Evan and I were outside under bright distant stars. "Maybe if we survive this," I suggested to Evan, "we could get a cabin in the mountains."

This is what all those well-meaning questions from concerned friends and family had been about, I realized. At the time, I had answered so full of confidence that we were prepared for the challenges of sailing. But now, suddenly, it was apparent how little control we had. For all the things I wanted in that moment — for the seas to be smaller, for our remaining rudder to stay strong — I also wanted to get to safety without my brave little sprite of a daughter absorbing my fear.

An endless day later, our 18th at sea, I saw a smudge on the horizon. That's what land looks like when you first spot it from the sea. And over the course of an hour I kept my eye on it — watching it take form and hold — ruling out cloud and squall. When I was sure of what I was seeing, I called Maia and Evan out on deck. I pointed to the patch of dark gray outlined against a background of medium gray and held Maia's finger as I traced the shape. "The Marquesas!?" she whispered excitedly.

Then she whooped a "Land Ho!" When she looked at her dad, she saw he had tears in his eyes. "But we found it. Why are you crying?"

A friend told me that an ocean crossing is like childbirth; the moment you step foot on land, you forget the pain and fear of getting there. As we made our way into the harbor at Nuka Hiva, the largest of the Marquesas Islands, glimpsing the mountain peaks through the morning mist and absorbing the intensity of the tropical green, I realized I didn't want to forget our passage.

The first step ashore after crossing an ocean doesn't come with traditions the way crossing the equator does. Some sailors kneel and kiss the earth, but most, like us, just sway with land sickness and feel overwhelmed by the smell of flowers and overripe fruit, and the cacophony of birds, kids and dogs. What I wanted to do once we finished the formalities of checking in with the local authorities was walk — maybe to get as far from our boat as I could. So together with our friends from our buddy boats, with whom we'd stayed in radio contact but hadn't seen since the start of the Pacific crossing, we climbed up through the heated jungle, legs shaking with the unfamiliar effort.

We were met on the trail by a Marquesan on horseback named Rue. He led us to a sacred site that was marked by huge banyan trees, sacrifice pits and Tiki statues. Evan and I pondered the ruins of stone pyramids and platforms, while Maia and the kids from our buddy boat ran around picking mangoes, star fruit and *pample-mousse* (grapefruit) from towering old trees. With fruit juice trickling down her freckled chin, Maia exclaimed that she'd never eaten anything so good. Everyone joked that this moment made the whole ocean-crossing thing worthwhile: standing in the sacred shade eating the best fruit in the world.

Breaking out of the jungle we reached the jagged cliffs that jutted over the ocean. Maia looked out over islands that faded into the distance and asked which we'd visit next. Evan and I looked back toward the harbor. From our vantage we could see boats belonging to some of the boldest ordinary people in the world. Ceilydh jumped out at me. Sailing her is like riding a magic carpet into a world I've always been intrigued by — she jumped out, not because she's more beautiful than the others, but because it's hard to sail a boat across an ocean and not fall a bit in love with her.

Even if she did throw a rudder.

Reaching for my hand, Evan asked how I felt about the cabin in the woods. "We'll fix the rudder," he told me. "We'll solve each problem that comes up." Half-listening to Maia as she chattered about the adventures we'd promised and the things she wanted to see, I looked out at the islands too. They were so beautiful, so mysterious, like a package on Christmas morning, just waiting to be opened.

We were different from that young couple who set off fearlessly on their first grand adventure. When we sailed away from the Marquesas with our new rudder, I felt tentative and cautious.

A few days later we dropped our anchor in the pristine water of a remote Tuamotu atoll and I watched Maia confidently leap into the ocean to get a better look at manta ray. I knew there would be risks as our family continued our sailing journey around the world, but we truly had an entire world to gain.

Diane Selkirk is a Canadian writer and photographer who's spent the past six years sailing around the world with her husband, daughter (now 13) and Charlie the cat. Along the way she's contributed stories to magazines that include National Geographic Travel, Reader's Digest, Men's Journal and Islands; newspapers such as The Washington Post, The Guardian and The Globe and Mail; and online websites including Outside, Slate, Travel + Leisure.com and the BBC.

THE END OF THE WORLD
Australia

I'd given up all hope of getting married by the time I met Henry Barley; I was 32 and had never before managed to have a serious long-term relationship. We met while I was filming a documentary in China of all places, even though we had been born less than a mile from each other and he went to school with my brother.

Henry fell in love with me when he saw me rescuing a hedgehog in a Chinese market. It had been bought for someone's supper and I bought it back and took it out into the countryside to set it free. I fell in love with him because he noticed; and helped me to do something that the rest of the film crew thought was stupid.

We had a paradise wedding in the Seychelles four months later, at the beginning of 1989, and both believed that life would follow the path of happy ever after. But five months later, Henry was diagnosed with terminal cancer and he died in my arms one year and 16 days after our wedding.

Despite the shock and horror, I'd be the first to admit that I probably had it relatively easy being a widow. After all, I'd only known Henry for 18 months so my previous life was still accessible. I can only imagine the crashing of worlds when a long-established marriage ends.

Even so, my future had been taken away — even more so because I had gambled my career by focusing on TV documentaries about China and, that very year, Tiananmen Square had destroyed that possibility. So I had no husband and no career.

Back in those days, before we had the habit of going to war in the Middle East and we got used to the shipping home of the bodies of young men, widowhood in your 30s was still quite an unusual thing and most people simply didn't know what to do with me.

I think the final straw was having supper with an old friend and he said "don't cry" when I shed some tears over my dessert. "Don't cry?" Two months after Henry died, don't cry? Of course he was trying to say it to comfort, but trust me, it didn't work.

I needed to be somewhere where I could begin to find "me" again on a blank canvas and I ran away to Australia for six weeks. You have to think clearly when you are somewhere new, and Australia was certainly that.

My family worried that I wasn't sane enough to be setting off for the unknown, but I'd previously spent six summers in China and adventure has always been my friend. This time it was going to be a life-saver. If I had to think on my feet, at least my thoughts would have some kind of positive focus.

I wasn't just jumping into the unknown alone; my long-term friends Peter Seccombe and Sarah Douglas were on a year's sabbatical traveling the world. They would be arriving in Australia just two months after Henry's death and we arranged for me to join them on the east coast.

My flight took me into Cairns in the Northern Territory and I arrived two days before Sarah and Pete could get there — in the days before mobile phones and the Internet when liaising on an exact date with travelers was a pretty tough call.

I arrived in Cairns the night before my 33rd birthday and was lucky to be allowed in, given that my Australian visa, which had arrived at the last minute, thought I'd be better named "Whitehorse" than "Whitehouse." It was a wonderful introduction to the Aussie state of mind that the immigration officer was happy to let me pet the beagle sniffing at my baggage while he pondered my passport. I told him about the beagle puppy who'd be greeting me when I got home and he decided that "what the heck, you're a dog-lover, not a smuggler. Welcome to Oz!"

Sarah and Pete hadn't arrived in Cairns yet; they were hoping to arrive within the next 48 hours so I had nothing to do but settle into my hotel room and walk around the town, which was mostly shut because it was a Sunday. There are only so many baths you can reasonably have in a day, so by 6 p.m. I was done and, tentatively, went down to the hotel bar with a book to pass an hour or two before deciding what and where to eat. I thought I'd have a glass of wine and read in a public place; you cry a lot less in public.

Within 15 minutes of my being there, a young Australian man threw himself into the seat next to me. I looked up, surprised, and he landed me with the worst chat-up line in the world.

"Me and my mates at the bar got a bet on," he said. "I bet them 10 bucks you can't be as mean as you look."

Actually, it worked. I was so nonplused and also so lonely that I talked to him, explaining why it was that I probably looked so unappealing. He was a true Aussie bloke and thought I should just cheer up and get on with things. After all, that's what Henry would want me to do, right? He managed to persuade me to go for a walk with him by the levée and we bought fish and chips, which we ate sitting by the water. Then we went to a broken-down bar and danced to a honky-tonk band, and that was both terrifying and incredible because, for the first time in two months, I felt life-force working in my body. Dancing was just what I needed to shake the misery from my soul.

But I went back to the hotel alone. My Aussie friend was quite sure that Henry wouldn't mind if I slept with him, but I had no such intention. I didn't even kiss him and he ended up being quite sure that he'd lost his bet. "You'd feel a lot better for a decent shag," he said.

I didn't agree. I was still holding the memory of Henry's body close to mine and wearing as many of his clothes that would fit — and which still retained his scent — and I felt guilty enough in the dark watches of the night for having had fun without him. But, even so, I'll always be grateful to my first Aussie friend for helping me through that first evening on the other side of the world.

It was my birthday the next day so I went out to the Barrier Reef to do some snorkeling. I had planned to wait until Sarah and Pete arrived but there are only so many circuits you can make of a town when you're miserable.

The ship that took us out was crowded with Japanese tourists so I could hide quite neatly in the crowd. I did listen to the announcements on where to swim and where not to go.

"Just avoid the deep water," said the announcer. "You're perfectly safe in the shallows and we keep an eye out for you. No one's ever been hurt in the shallows but you must stay there because there are sharks in the deep water, and two divers were killed by a giant barracuda only about six weeks ago. That guy wasn't within 20 miles of here, but it's best to be sure."

Into the water we all went and I floundered around for a while, hating it. My mind wasn't relaxed enough to deal with all the shouting, giggling and photograph-taking all around me. What did I do? Yes, of course I swam round the boat. I had completely forgotten what the announcer said.

The barracuda was right there, lurking. It was enormous, with great black marks like portholes down its side and teeth that made me shiver. It was side on when I first saw it, but it flipped in less than a second to face-on and came toward me so fast it was like a blur.

It's true that time slows down in a crisis. I remember the terror — and I also remember thinking very clearly, "I want to live." Until that moment, I hadn't been sure.

A voice cut into my thoughts very clearly. "Swim forward and make as much noise as you can. When you get near, hit it on the nose. If it turns, poke its eye with your thumb."

So I did the complete opposite of what instinct wanted me to do — swim away as fast as possible — and obeyed the Voice without thought. I swam straight at the barracuda, yelling under the water.

It flipped away.

I lay there and watched it; it watched me. What did I do next? The Voice suggested, "You could swim backward." I never knew I could do that but I could! When my legs touched the side of the ship I turned and swam around it as fast as I could. Just as I had the protective body of the ship behind me, I remembered that I had an underwater camera. With journalistic instinct and the fear that no one would believe my incredible story without proof, I risked pointing the camera around the boat and took a picture of the now-distant fish. Out of the water, I retched with fear and shook like a leaf.

I didn't tell anyone on the ship; I was too scared of being told off, and there was no one else who was about to be as stupid as I had been. But as I sat, wrapped in my towel, shivering, I knew: I wanted to live. Henry's death was not the end of me and I would survive.

I have the murky, slightly out-of-focus photograph of that barracuda on the desktop of my computer to look at whenever I'm feeling small or scared. It helps.

Sarah and Pete arrived in Cairns the next day with a sturdy 4x4 automobile to take us north into the Daintree National Forest, Cape Tribulation and beyond to Cook-town. The name of the Cape is, perhaps, a suitable warning. It is where the 18th century explorer Capt. James Cook's ship, Endeavour, hit the reef and, as he said, "the start of all their troubles" (mostly sickness) from there on.

There's also Point Danger, where the Tweed River empties into the sea, and Mount Warning, so he wasn't feeling in the best of spirits as he discovered this new land, and I could understand why.

Australia is full of things that really want to attack you and, quite frequently, kill you. There are the legend-ary spiders for a start — the Funnel-Web, the Redback, the Mouse Spider, Fiddlebacks, Tarantulas and even the Trapdoor Spider, whose bite can give you lethargy and nausea if nothing worse.

There are deadly Taipan and Brown snakes and death adders, and the sea is no better. The box jellyfish will kill you as soon as they look at you at certain times of the year, and the cone shells, the blue-ringed octopus and sundry other fearsome beasts lie in wait to cause serious damage. The sand flies on the beaches aren't much fun either.

And that's not even mentioning the saltwater crocodiles — or the sharks.

On the yuck-but-harmless side, the cockroaches are enormous.

In addition, there are plants that will attack you, too. I went horse riding in the dappled, steamy forest of Daintree National Park and encountered the Wait-a-While or Layer plant — a kind of vine with thorns that will happily catch on your clothing or snag your skin, causing it to bleed, as you pass (very ouch when encountered with bare arms while cantering!).

But it was wonderful to be with dear friends in the most beautiful land. No, Sarah and Pete could not replace Henry, but they were a constant, life-enhancing presence and, as a threesome, we had that precious resource of one of us being in the back seat of the car to have some alone time.

There were still many nights when I cried myself to sleep but, in Queensland, there was always a tomorrow of something new, something to experience, to appreciate or even to be slightly scared of.

We drove north and took the ferry across the Daintree River into a lush and sensual tumbling of trees and plants, streams and creeks, calling birds and frogs, and with a soft, humid sheen that lifted the temperature into the high 80s.

At Port Douglas, with its lovely hotels (we stayed in a hostel but had access to a wonderful swimming pool), Pete and I went out to the Barrier Reef again. Sarah wasn't a confident swimmer.

I was scared. Even getting into the water was hard, but there was a hand to hold mine — and it did help that it was a comforting male hand — and he waited in the water with me until I was ready and willing to put my face below the slightly choppy waves.

Together we swam in a paradise of beauty over the reef surrounded by yellow butterfly fish, purple and green parrot fish, clown fish, angel fish, bright blue damsel and surgeonfish, stripy triggerfish and the great grey hump-crowned wrasse.

Not one sign of anything scary, just beauty and life-force.

Swimming in coral is never quite as bright as you will see it on the TV — they are using lights with which to film — but it is still a rainbow of colors. You're not supposed to feed the fish (and we didn't) but I remembered taking bread out into the waters of the Seychelles with Henry and how eagerly the fish had taken it from our hands, their mouths hard and blunt against our skin.

Back on the road north, we took the un-tarmacked road from Port Douglas north to Cooktown. Several times we took detours down mud tracks and graveled surfaces, fording rivers, watching turtles "plop" into waters to escape us, and gazing up through the canopy of glittering green at flashes of color of unidentified tropical birds.

On one road we even cut back the branches of a fallen tree and forded a river up to the base of the doors before being stopped by a rock fall. All silly, pointless adventures — and great fun.

Then we got a puncture and discovered that the spare tire, too, was flat. Fortunately, we were just outside Cooktown so all we had to do was limp a few hundred yards into the main street and call the car hire company, which promised to send two new tires by sea, taking up to three days.

We didn't do a lot in Cooktown while we waited for the tires to be shipped to us from Cairns because back in 1989 there wasn't a lot to do. In Cairns, they had described the people of Cooktown as "ornery," which didn't mean unpleasant but seemed to mean parochial and with rather closely-related families. I have no evidence of that being true at all.

At the mouth of the Endeavour River, Cooktown was the gateway to Australia's gold-mining region. Nowadays it's thriving, with a bitumen road from Cairns, but when we were there even the main street was rough and the greatest prosperity seemed to come from the shrimp boats.

It's a tropical town and the hostel where we stayed had its fair share of giant cockroaches and cane toads, so we spent much of the time resting and reading in the local pub where we ate crocodile (which tasted like slightly tough fishy chicken) and kangaroo (which tasted like slightly rabbity chicken). To our great surprise, after 24 hours, the bar staff started giving us drinks on the house.

Granted, Australians — and Northern Queenslanders in particular — are very friendly, but this is not normal. So we started asking questions. It turns out they had a lingerie show coming up in four days and, given that Sarah and I were the slimmest girls currently in town, they were hoping to persuade us to take part as models...

They were certainly confused about our status: one man with two Sheilas. Were we both with him? It had to be so because there seemed no other explanation. But if one of us were available, which was it? Bets were on at the bar.

Pete gave it away when he stopped a bonzer bloke from chatting Sarah up, but let a guy get me a drink, so after that I was fair game. I hate to think what the local girls thought, but in the days of the unsealed road there weren't that many female strangers in town, and new blood is always popular.

The second-worst chat-up line in the world happened in that bar. Now that I think of it, it doesn't seem that bad, but the guy was only my height, had a couple of gold teeth and several days' beard before it was fashionable. He sat on a chair backwards and said, "You wanna come out to my shrimp boat? It's got a shower."

It was dark; his shrimp boat was moored in the estuary and the only way to get to it would be to swim in the crocodile-infested river.

I don't think you have to work very hard to anticipate my (very polite) reply.

We didn't stay for the lingerie show, and when the tires arrived we headed south again. I do wish now that we had gone farther north into the Northern Territories, but I will always remember with great love my time in Queensland and the men who, if they didn't manage to date me, certainly made me laugh and to realize that, when my heart had mended, there would be new life and the possibility of new love ahead of me.

The Rev. Maggy Whitehouse is a former BBC World Service journalist and independent television documentaries producer, as well as a prolific author on Bible history and metaphysics. She was ordained in 2007 and trained as a stand-up comedian in 2012. She works throughout the UK as a storyteller, minister, inspirational speaker and comedian.

A TALE OF TWO SOUPS
Spain

For years, my father would tell me about this soup.

"Best soup I ever had in my life," he'd say, before re-telling the story as if we hadn't heard it 400 times. He remembered every detail, from the ingredients in the soup to the song playing in the background (Simon & Garfunkel's "El Condor Pasa") to the books my mother was reading when they were traveling around southern Spain as newlyweds (Hemingway — all of them).

This is a man who misplaces his glasses several times daily and still isn't entirely sure when my birthday is. If one 43-year-old meal could leave such an impression on that least reliable of memories, I had to hunt it down and try it for myself.

The year was 1970. The place, he swore, was Mála-ga, the Mediterranean port city on Spain's Costa del Sol and birthplace of Pablo Picasso. The name of the restau-

rant inconveniently escapes him now; he remembers only that they had to hike up a mountain to arrive at a
fancy hotel "with a fantastic view of the Rock of Gibraltar." He and my mother, being young and relatively
broke, could only afford the cheapest dish on the menu:
a simple yet elegant soup made from cream, shellfish
and sherry.

My father's memory of this soup may be vividly detailed, but detail doesn't always mean accuracy.
Periodically I'd break out a map and agonize over the
unresolvable dissonance: Málaga is 139 kilometers from
Gibraltar, two hours by car, with a nub of land sticking
out in between. I Googled "Can you see the Rock of Gibraltar from Málaga?" but the results were inconclusive.
Was he positive it was Málaga? Was it, possibly, Mar-
bella, the resort town on the other side of the nub, closer
to Gibraltar and perhaps a likelier tourist destination in
the '70s? No, it was Málaga, he was sure.

*****

It was dark when I arrived in Málaga on the bus from
Granada, too dark to get the lay of the land. I checked
into my *pensione*, a huge, creaky old house decked out
in tacky tchotchkes and overseen by a charmingly eccentric innkeeper. As she led me past porcelain cat figurines
and two ominous-looking suits of armor keeping sentry
in the hall, I asked her: "Is there a mountain here? With a
hotel on the top?"

Her face screwed into a question mark, and I tried to explain my mission in imperfect Spanish: the honey-mooners, the long hike up the hill, the best soup ever.

A look of recognition registered on her face, and she started talking fast in a mostly indecipherable Andaluz accent. (In this part of Spain they're known for "eating their letters," forcing tourists to interpret that a word like "Graaaaaaaaaa" actually means "Granada.") One thing she said caught my ear: Gibralfaro.

Gibralfaro? That's almost like Gibraltar, both names rooted in the Arabic "Jebel," meaning "mountain." Could it be that my dad had mixed up the names and I was in the right place after all, one step closer to tasting this fabled soup?

The next morning I set out for Mount Gibralfaro, which rises above the center of town and is crowned with an imposing castle fortress; at its foot are the ruins of a 2,000-year-old Roman amphitheater and an Arabic palace called the Alcazaba. Málaga is one of the world's oldest cities, dating to at least the 8th century B.C. The Alcazaba was built by the Moors on the site of an ancient Phoenician settlement to shield the town from skirmishes that broke out as the Caliphate of Córdoba began to crumble in the 11th century. However, 500 years later, the fortifications did little to protect Málaga from Gen. Francisco Franco, whose Nationalist forces took the city during the Spanish Civil War, killing several thousand civilians. The structures survived, and today tourists marvel at the Alcazaba's multifoil arches, intricately carved interiors and tranquil gardens.

As I ascended the steep switchbacks leading up the mountain from the Alcazaba, I wasn't surprised to discover that there is no view of the Rock of Gibraltar — only the Costa del Sol's dramatic hilly coastline disappearing into the mist to the south and the busy seaport stretching out below. I imagined the view wasn't so different from the one my parents would have seen in 1970, when towns all along this section of coast were built up during Spain's tourism boom. Midcentury-era apartment towers loomed over a marina filled with expensive yachts. I could see Málaga's perfectly round bullring, dropped in the center of town like a cookie-cutter. I wondered if this was the site of the bullfight my mother insisted my dad take her to see during her "Death in the Afternoon" phase, only to run from the building in tears after the first match.

My parents were probably just the kind of business Franco was going for when he claimed he wanted to turn the Costa del Sol into "the Florida of Europe." In one of his few positive legacies, Franco expanded Spain's investment in the *paradors*, government-owned hotels meant to attract tourism to historic sites and pay for their upkeep — there's one inside the Alhambra and another awaiting me in the castle atop Gibralfaro. The Parador of Málaga opened in 1948 and now features an arcaded stone facade, sprawling views, a swimming pool — and,

I hoped, a certain soup that would make this whole trip worthwhile.

Sweaty and breathless from the climb, I approached the hotel and crumpled into a chair next to an outside table set up near the edge of an overlook. Scanning the menu, my heart sank. The lone soup listed — a gazpacho — was definitely not the one my father had raved about all these decades.

When the waitress came, I explained my plight: "*Mi papá ... hace 43 años ... mejor sopa de su vida ... con mariscos y crema y jerez.*"

Before I could finish, she nodded and said, "*Gazpachuelo malagueño.*" It is, apparently, a signature of the region and the hotel, normally served only in the posh upstairs dining room, but she would see if they could make an exception for me, clad as I was in jeans and sneakers.

Fifteen minutes later, two waiters arrived. One carried a gleaming silver cloche, and when he lifted the lid it revealed a shallow white plate upon which was arranged a single clam, a mussel, a sliver of fish, a few chunks of potato and a slice of bread. The other server held a matching silver tureen, from which he ladled a pale yellow broth, scented with the aroma of sherry, which is produced a few provinces over in Jerez de la Frontera.

Gazpachuelo malagueño is like a Mediterranean version of clam chowder, only served at room temperature. The first taste was ... underwhelming. This was the best soup my dad ever ate? I was tempted to ask for a salt shaker. With each spoonful, though, I grew to appreciate the subtleties of the flavor, the way the tender mussel's briny burst played off the potato's starch, and how beautifully the sweet-and-acid sherry balanced the rich stock. The creaminess of the soup, it turns out, doesn't come from cream at all but from homemade mayonnaise, which is integrated into the seafood broth ever-so-carefully to avoid curdling.

It's a fine soup, good enough that I asked for the recipe, and have attempted it at home several times since. But what made it the best soup of my dad's life probably had more to do with the intoxication of being young and in love than with the sherry. Food was just the catalyst that encoded the experience into his brain and fixed it there all these years. Similarly, I was driven to retrace his steps less by epicurean curiosity than by the thrill of the hunt, the satisfaction of solving the mystery of a muddled memory.

It's always been this way in my family, the memories inextricably bound up with food. Nobody can really recall whether we went to church on Easter, but everybody remembers the bright orange tub of Schuler's cheese and the kielbasa Grandma would bring from the Polish deli to serve at Easter brunch. Trying to remember my 30th birthday dinner party is like looking at an old photograph: the features of the people seated at the table a little fuzzy, the exact creaminess of the seared scallop in sharp focus.

Sometimes I worry that there is something mildly pathological about this — and maybe there is. What matters is that a memory gets made, inaccurate or impressionistic though it may be. A simple thing like soup can be remembered and passed down like an heirloom. I hope in 40 years I'm telling my kids about the best soup I ever had in my life, and what a nice view the restaurant had of the Rock of Gibraltar.

Maya Kroth has written about nostalgic soups, artisanal puppets, eccentric Tijuana architects, cardboard movie-set towns in the desert, southern barbecue, Honduran economics, Guatemalan lake pollution, Al Capone and more, for outlets including Foreign Policy, theatlantic.com, The Christian Science Monitor and The Washington Post. She splits her time between San Diego, Mexico City and Kalamazoo, MI.

GETTING THE HANG OF LOVE
Switzerland

I am standing at the edge of a steep precipice, my wobbly legs protesting and knees knocking together like the prongs of a tuning fork. Never before has vertigo seemed so real. Never before has my comfortable chair at home seemed less boring. Strapped into various harnesses and helmets and other things, I am beginning to fully appreciate the "gravity" of the situation. I scarcely have time to contemplate what is starting to look like a foolishly hasty decision before being instructed on what to do and how to do it.

However, I am too busy concentrating on being able to breathe properly. I take one look at the pitifully inadequate piece of fiber and shudder, fervently hoping it can hold my not inconsiderable weight. Eventually, belts are tightened, buckles are clasped and ropes are tugged, and a feeble voice calls out from the distance to start running.

*****

"Mix a little French highbrow with a little German stiff upper lip with a little Italian style and get a heady whiff of fantastic Switzerland!"

The promotional pitch jumps out from the center-spread advertisement of a travel agency in bright bold inviting letters. My boyfriend peeps out from behind the poster. "So, what do you think?" I blink and gaze at the photographs. Tall stately mountain peaks tower over a city twinkling with night lights. Pristine white slopes reflect sunlight like polished mirrors as happy families cavort on skis making designer tracks in the virgin snow. Freshly mowed, nature-defying green gardens drip dew while children pose at picnic tables and couples sit under secluded overhanging palm fronds whispering romantic sweet nothings to each other. Everything, right down to the artistically placed pebbles on cobbled roads, appears to be tempting the poor excluded reader to hurry on over and share a piece of the pie.

"I think," I say slowly, "that it's all air-brushed to give a good effect. The children look scruffy and I am pretty sure the mountains are painted on. And I can't tell if the people are smiling or grimacing, especially those couples."

Running a critical eye over it I shake my head, glance at my boyfriend and return to reading my book.

A wistful sigh escapes his lips. "Um, I was hoping..."

"Yes?"

"That we could, maybe, go on a brief vacation."

I give a cynical sniff. My boyfriend knows that sniff. It can mean anything from "Nothing" (usually in answer to his "What's the matter?") to "You are being completely unreasonable" to "I want an ice cream and I want it right now" to "Go away, I have a headache." This time, however, it meant "Don't be absurd. I have no time for your jokes." It pretty much silenced him on the subject for the rest of the day. I'll say this for my boyfriend, he certainly knows when he is beaten.

*****

As a computer programmer, I normally lead a sedentary life. Outdoor activity is limited to the weekly run from home to the supermarket. And that is how I like it. I am perfectly at home with my books, my computer and my broadband connection, which does all the traveling for me from the convenience of my couch. Being placid to the point of boring, I am not one of those people who goes looking for adventure. However, on this occasion the lure of the broadsheet proves to be too strong. Besides, I love my boyfriend and am aware that I won't be able to rest in peace having seen that disappointed look on his face.

The next morning, feeling just that bit of reckless intrepidness that lends itself to such things, I have summoned courage enough to take the plunge. I make all the arrangements in secret and, that night, over an elaborate candlelight dinner, I take his hand, ask him to close his eyes and place a thick bundle of tickets on his palm. His expression of surprise, changing to dawning comprehension and then to utter delight is worth all the effort and more than compensates for my nervousness that has already begun to lurk in the background.

Our destination is Interlaken, a panoramic city of kaleidoscopic hues. With the majestic Alps at its doorstep, Interlaken specializes in adventure sports: canyon-ing, white water rafting, bungee jumping. There is something here for everyone. Trembling with excitement (or is it fear?) we find ourselves embarking a week later upon an adventure that promises to give us a high — tandem paragliding.

At the appointed hour, we reach the foot of the hill where introductions are in progress. While boyfriend wanders off to check out all the cool gear, I ask the instructor-pilots how long they have been paragliding. Michelle replies, "I've been doing this for 16 years." I hide my relief at this assurance and pretend not to get alarmed when we're asked to fill out a battery of forms, all of which want to know our next of kin. As our little convoy proceeds up the incline, boyfriend saunters along easily while I huff and puff like a steam engine, then progress to sounding like a herd of steam engines and then a herd of steam engines with labor pains. Eventually we come upon the savior of all mankind — the pickup van. Within minutes we have loaded our gear into it and are off to the summit.

Before long, I find myself high atop a mountain perched like an eagle with its wings clipped, trying not to move around too much for fear that I'll fall off the edge. I try to keep up with the take-off and landing instructions but am unable to grasp more than the rudimentary principles involved. I am also dismayed to learn that boyfriend and I will be flying separately. A quick peck on the lips and an encouraging smile and he is off, strong, sure legs pounding on the ground, a final crouch, a powerful spring and the paraglider mushrooms open gracefully like a slow-motion blooming flower.

A hop, skip and jump later, I am away too — flying gloriously like a bird, a tiny speck in the sky. Astonished at having taken off so smoothly, I can't stop gaping. Then I come to my senses and snap my mouth shut. Any lower and my jaw would have gotten a literal taste of "ground reality."

The wind picks up and throws us higher, and the glider buffets around for a moment like a twig in a tornado. Gak! I should have called my lawyer to make my will. I squeeze my eyes shut and hoarsely croak a small prayer. When I open my eyes, cool white mists are swirling all around.

Is this Heaven?

From somewhere above my right ear a voice sounding like Michelle's booms, "There is so much fog here."

Oh, ah.

When we eventually break clear of the cloud cover we find ourselves flying high above Lake Thun, with the city spread out below us like a map. I can see a train snaking its way into the railway station. Oh the thrill! Oh the glorious excitement! Oh the, groan, nausea that threatens to engulf me like a tidal wave!

Emitting enough shrieks to be mistaken for a mobile aviary, I forget my initial nervousness and revel in the sensation of floating. The fiber of the paraglider rustles sharply and the thermals lift us higher. To my left I can see the distinctive colors of boyfriend's paraglider doing audacious stunts like spiraling and weaving. It makes me dizzy. Michelle notices my anxious glances and reassures me. "It's absolutely safe. Do you want to try it?"

"No, thank you," I squeak.

Down below, Lake Brienz resembles a blot of spilled pale blue ink. A great fear suddenly seizes me — what if we fall into the water? I can't swim! No, of course not, admonishes a nasty little voice inside my head. We eventually pass onto land once more without mishap.

A bright streak of color zooms into my thoughts as a bird flies by. I don't know which of us is more startled.

Suddenly boyfriend is in front of me, having persuaded his pilot to maneuver his glider directly onto our path. "What are you doing? Are you out of your mind?"

I yell in fright, afraid that our gliders may get entangled and we'll both plummet to our deaths.

He grins and opens his mouth. Out pop the last words I would have expected to hear here. "Devyani, will you marry me?"

Time seems to stop. A moment ago the wind was rushing around me, and now it has gone pin-drop quiet. Indeed, the wind seems to have been knocked out of me. I can't believe what I've heard, yet I have never been so certain of anything. The pilots are forgotten, the paragliders are forgotten, the fact that we are about five miles straight up in the air hanging in open empty space is forgotten. All that I am aware of is this man in front of me who loves me enough to want to spend the rest of his life with me. My throat is choked. I can only whisper, "Yes." It is enough. There is no need to shout. He knows, and I know he knows. The moment passes as Michelle congratulates me and my boyfriend, smiles and flamboyantly whirls away.

We are airborne for 12 incredible minutes. Still, when the time comes for us to descend, neither of us is too unwilling. Not for me a tame landing, though.

"We will have to land in the wrong direction of the air current," Michelle yells over the roar of the wind. "Can you run fast?"

As the earth rushes up to meet our feet, we are unable to keep up with the momentum of the paraglider at touch-down and, in a most undignified conclusion, my pilot and I fall over backward. We are dragged several feet on the lawn, no doubt irreparably marring the grass beds. But having enough layers of clothing on to give competition to a rhinoceros, I am unhurt — shaken, but not freaking out any more than usual. Michelle emerges unscathed too, having had the good sense to keep me below her at all times.

Boyfriend, who has already landed comfortably, rushes over as soon as he can shrug free of his glider. His face is pale with concern and his eyes sick with worry. He is looking daggers at the pilots and thinking murderous thoughts even though it isn't exactly their fault. After I reaffirm again and again that I am all right, he helps me out of the various contraptions and we help the pilots roll up the paragliders. "Real sorry about that, folks," Michelle says in a genuinely apologetic voice. "Usually it is a cakewalk, but, hey, Mother Nature, you know. So unpredictable." We console ourselves with shrugs, grinning proudly for the cameras.

On the flight back, I take one last look at the Alps standing tall and proud — a symbol of life and unfettered enjoyment. I look into the loving eyes of my better half, give him an affectionate smile and lay my head on his capable shoulders. He gives me an absent-minded pat. Observing the far-away look in his eyes, I'm sure that he is already planning our next trip. But as far as I am concerned, we are both about to set out on the biggest adventure of our lives — together.

Devyani Borade writes on the humor and pathos of everyday life. Her fiction, nonfiction and art have appeared in magazines throughout the world. She likes to eat chocolates, read comic books and try her husband's patience. Visit her website Verbolatry at devyaniborade.blogspot.com.

THREADS TO THE PAST
China

This is not going well. The orphanage director, Mr. Li, takes his seat without introducing himself or welcoming us, and our interpreter, Grace, immediately fires off a question: Can we see my daughter's file, as promised by a previous director almost 10 years ago?

I'd planned to build to this subject over time, after a little friendly small talk. But now the question has bulleted across the table, and Mr. Li responds with what sounds like a firm and final pronouncement.

Neither Sophie nor I speak much Chinese. She has taken classes for a month and can say, "This is my nose." I took a class many years ago and retain little, except the sentence, "I am not a doctor": "*Wa bu shi dai-fu.*" I remember this so well because Gubo, the guy on the language tape, spat out the words as if furiously offended that anyone would dare to mistake him for a doctor. I can still imitate his tones and inflections, which I did a bit hesitantly for our guide in Beijing a few days ago when she asked me if I spoke any Chinese. I half-expected her to rear back at my unnecessarily forceful rejection of the medical profession, but instead she looked impressed and made me repeat it for a guide at a silk factory, who also looked impressed. "We can understand you," they both said approvingly.

Since then, Sophie and I have been proudly throwing around our Chinese, getting endless mileage out of this one sentence: "I'd help people who are suffering, but *wa bu shi daifu*," Sophie might announce casually, to which I'd reply, "I would have started us on the antibiotics sooner, but *wa bu shi daifu*."

My daughter sags in the leather seat next to me, her mouth a network of wires and bands that are red this month in honor of China. Her gaze drifts to the elaborate grates over windows that look out across a courtyard to the baby room where she once slept. She is zoning out at this important long-awaited meeting, still recovering from the stomach bug that stranded us in Chengdu an extra day.

I listen intently as if I can follow the conversation. Grace speaks, then Mr. Li, Grace, and Mr. Li again.

A negotiation appears to be unfolding, and hope fills me: Maybe Grace will coax out of Mr. Li a piece of my daughter's past. But then Grace turns to us and reduces 10 minutes of conversation to three words: "He says no."

"Show him the picture," Grace says, with no transition, before I've had a chance to recover from my disappointment. I haven't steeled myself yet for more pleas or arguments, head shakes or buttoned lips.

But I nod at Sophie and she slides the picture, sealed in a Ziploc bag, across the table. It's a photo of us almost 10 years ago, me, a red-cheeked baby and a man, a nameless man we've always referred to as The Man. In the picture we are all smiling. The Man holds the baby and shakes a plastic rattle, a colorful cage enclosing jingle bells that bounce up and down.

I have shown this picture to Sophie many times, telling her the story: The Man, probably a member of the orphanage staff, had brought her on a train to me at my hotel in Hangzhou. She'd hung on to him tightly. Gently, he'd peeled her fist from his shirt and thrust her into my arms. Huge tears pooled in her eyes. As he retreated, her hands strained urgently toward him, fingers twitching, and I felt like a kidnapper. All night she howled operatically, her quick dark eyes distrustful. In the morning when The Man came to say goodbye, she tucked her head joyfully into his shoulder. He jingled the rattle and her laughter trilled, itself like little bells.

The Man was the one I wanted to talk to when the interpreter was free. Who are you? I wanted to ask. Why are you so important to her? But The Man stepped aside for my interview with the orphanage director, filled with vague pleasantries about good sleeping habits and favorite foods. It became distressingly clear that he didn't know a single particular about my sleepless baby with only two teeth. Then, in the chaos of paperwork, baby foot and handprints stamped in ink on thin paper, an appearance before a judge in which I vowed to provide for this baby and never abuse or abandon her, I lost sight of The Man.

Because current laws in China make attempts to track birthparents potentially dangerous for them, the story of The Man may always be one of the only narrow threads we have connecting my daughter to her past. I have used the picture as my fragile bit of evidence that someone loved her the first few months of her life. Should we risk new information that might reconfigure this story? What if The Man was a stranger who smelled familiar to her, like sticky white rice and jasmine tea and cigarettes? What if he was just some man who was good with babies? What if he is only a comforting myth I invented? After all, I have a picture of the orphanage staff that I have examined carefully, unable to find him.

The orphanage director snaps the picture off the table like a playing card and deals it back to us with only a cursory glance. His answer is quicker this time. All the staff has changed in the last 10 years. The Man's face is not familiar. And with that, it seems, our quest is over. With that, finally and forever, our myths are intact but so much has been lost: my daughter's first smile, the first time she rolled over, crammed her fist in her mouth, laughed, cut a tooth, gripped a caretaker's finger and guided it to her mouth to slobber and gnaw. With the words of the orphanage director, all of those missing moments have been fully erased.

*****

At the other end of the table laid out with plates of oranges and small crisp green fruits like tiny apples, Mr. Yu, our driver, leaps up. He strides from the room. Cigarette break, I think. Mr. Li waits in his characteristic formal silence for my next question.

We are like unprepared hikers at high altitudes. My daughter's eyes glaze. I feel sluggish and droopy. Sophie has no questions, or if she does, she's either too bored or intimidated to ask them. I frame obligatory ones and avoid looking at my watch as I try to prolong the interview to a respectable length. Then we can visit the baby room, shop for items to donate, and return to our hotel. How many children live in the orphanage, what are their ages, how many will be adopted, where do the older ones go to school? What else can I ask, and how soon can we gracefully depart?

Mr. Yu bursts back into the room. Over the days of driving us, he has shown a slightly paternal affection toward Sophie. And now he's talking fast, smiling big enough to show his nicotine-stained teeth. The director stiffens. Grace blinks. Her eyes open wider. She leans forward. Sophie and I glance at each other, waiting for a translation, but now everybody's talking at once. We will just have to wait.

*****

A few days ago, in a soft sleeper train from Beijing to Xi'an, I woke early. Plunging behind a heavy curtain reeking of smoke, I watched China go by, mountains backed by a pink sunrise, silver rails shimmering alongside us, bok choy fields and apple orchards and low buildings sliding by. Then the curtains had been whisked open to let in the light and we were peeling and sharing oranges, and rattling newspapers. In the corridor, a hubbub of morning voices arose, a child singing and chanting, people trooping to the washroom in slippers carrying toiletry kits. Cigarette smoke filled the car.

I am reminded now of that seamless switch from peaceful silence and sleepy confusion to a chaos of activity, because whatever is going on in the orphanage meeting room has nudged everyone into a similar state of wide-awake animation. They all pitch forward like passengers about to reach their station. Mr. Yu's words sizzle and crackle, sparklers igniting Grace and even Mr. Li, who are talking at the same time. Mr. Yu repeatedly pounds his arm with the heel of his hand. Sophie whispers, "I think he's saying, 'Cut off my arm! Just cut off my arm!'"

But it turns out that Mr. Yu doesn't require an emergency amputation, nor is he threatening to sacrifice a limb if the director doesn't try a little harder. Mr. Yu has taken matters into his own hands and gone to talk to the staff, and one of them identified The Man. They know his wife. But The Man and his wife have both retired to the countryside, far away. Grace sounds regretful. It is unlikely that we will find The Man, she says.

"Wait here," Grace says, and she and Mr. Yu and Mr. Li retreat to an office down the hall. Soon they are back with a colorful laminated map and four more members of the staff. Everyone's interrupting, overlapping, gesturing and peering over Mr. Yu's shoulder as he stabs at locations on the map and traces distances with his finger.

"It is very far," Grace says. Small worry lines furrow her brow. "Do you really want to go look for The Man?"

*****

I wanted this trip to help Sophie feel connected to her past, but maybe just being in China will have to be enough. She has sipped tea with chrysanthemum petals floating on top and rock sugar melting on the bottom. She has flown a kite in Tiananmen Square and observed fifth-grade gym and English classes at a school in the Hutong. Wearing rubber gloves, she petted the stiff fur of a giant panda while it devoured fresh bamboo. She feels a sense of belonging in China that I can't fully understand. I feel left out of her longing for a world so different from the one I can offer, but still pleased that a little of her home country, a missing part of her, has been restored.

I wish it were enough that she now belongs to a family that dotes on her, that she and I share Grace as a middle name, that she is a part of my line now, set to inherit the crystal bowl passed down to all the Graces in my family. It seems auspicious that the western name of our interpreter here in Yiwu is also Grace. Maybe my daughter will never know who her birthmother or birthfather are, what they look like, what they have endured. But maybe, just maybe, there are other things she can know. So when Grace says, "Do you really want to go find The Man?" and Sophie shifts out of her daydream to answer, "Yes," I nod my assent.

And with that, the day spins entirely out of my control. We pile into the van, Sophie and I, Grace and Mr. Yu, and a young orphanage worker named Mr. Feng who knows a shortcut. Infectious with laughter and anticipation and goodwill, we go careening down the highway so fast that my pictures I'm taking out the window, even using the motion stabilizer, are blurred. But I snap one after the other, recording this countryside: rows of small colored flags flying from roofs; bikes pulling wooden wagons; road workers in wide-brimmed straw hats; mulberry, camphor and willow trees; fields of sugar cane and rice; red lanterns hanging from stores; farmers' houses with towers and turrets and shiny windows, carefully detailed and freshly painted, looking cut from gingerbread. And ducks on a pond, haystacks tied at the top like witches' brooms, an occasional pagoda on a hill, mountains folding over each other in the distance.

Dusty heat blows through the van and everyone shouts words I don't understand but with a cadence and volume and pitch I do, words wrought with a touching eagerness to offer something to this skinny American girl in braces and a faded T-shirt from a gymnastics meet.

For an hour, Mr. Yu starts and stops crazily. He forces the van between two cars as confidently as if our vehicle were a motorbike. The cars part to create a third lane on the two-lane highway. We bounce along in our newly-created lane, off on an adventure or maybe a fool's errand, in search of a mythical face in a picture, someone who might remember the girl nodding off in the back seat, a man who once loosened her small hand from his shirt and placed it gently in my hand as if to say, here, she is yours now, while his eyes flickered as if with regretful determination. Based on expressions and gestures I might have misread, based on a baby's giggle and grip 10 years ago, we are flying down the highway to locate a stranger, veering down another road and into the countryside in search of The Man.

*****

We pull up on the shoulder of a dusty road. Below us, beside a pond, a woman lowers a pair of pants, pushing it into the water, then lifting the cloth, heavy, to flatten it on a rock. Water laps peacefully as she dips each garment. As we walk away, loud noises erupt: whop, whop, whop. She has laid out all the wet laundry on rocks and is beating it with a stick. The sound carries across the silent village.

Grace opens an umbrella to protect against the sun and we head down narrow roads the width of alleys between old brick and plaster buildings with ceramic roofs. Yellow flecks of rice have been spread out to dry along the walks. A woman in a broad-brimmed straw hat rakes them, creating furrows between the long rows. We take care not to step on them.

The Man has a name, Lu Xing Qian, Mr. Lu. Grace fills me in as we walk. He is a wealthy merchant from Yiwu, whose wife once worked at the orphanage. Wealthy means that he owns a shop, two cars and a house in the city. He also maintains a place in this village where he is building a retirement home.

Mr. Feng goes to knock on the door of Mr. Lu's building. We wait on the sidewalk. I will the door to open, but it doesn't. A scrawny black lab skitters from the entryway. "He's not home," Grace tells us. "But this is his pet dog."

Mr. Feng is undeterred by the empty apartment. He briskly leads us on, down more roads, around more corners, past trees and crops and silos and cell phone towers, and houses crowded together. There is no traffic but the occasional motorbike, none of the hum and roar of airplanes and cars and appliances and radios that underscores the air of cities, just this remote silence.

Finally we reach the construction site of Mr. Lu's new house. It's a depression in the dirt with steel rods shooting out, a crane perched alongside, bricks stacked on the edge. No one is here. Mr. Feng climbs over hills of gravel and heads down a slope. I jump at a sound, a flap of wings as a rooster leaps from the fence behind me. And then, up through the hills of gravel comes a triumphant Mr. Feng, followed by two people. I recognize the woman from photos of the orphanage staff. The Man is the picture in my hand come to life, his kind face a bit more aged, his waistline slightly more expanded.

I'm not sure how old he is, maybe 50s or early 60s. I hand him the picture, but he returns it with barely a glance. He does not need a picture, this gesture seems to say. Of course he remembers Ni Qiao Qin.

"He recognizes you," Grace tells me. "But not her. She has changed so much."

Now it is time to inspect Sophie. She has become used to this ritual. She stands patiently, slightly bemused, as everyone congregates to admire her and pronounce her a "very nice girl," according to Grace's translation. We smile a lot. We pose with the Lus and take pictures.

Then Mr. Feng and Mr. Lu decide that we will all have lunch, and so we crowd into the van, seven of us now, and drive to an open-air restaurant, the roof held up by bamboo posts. A waitress brings mugs of beer and for Sophie and me, Sunny D. For a good 15 minutes, our hosts and driver and interpreter all toast us and each other, refilling our glasses constantly. Our stomachs are sloshing with Sunny D by the time the mayor of the town arrives at our table to thank us for visiting and propose a toast. We smile and raise our glasses again.

We drink tea and snap sunflower seeds, piling up heaps of shells. I want to ask questions: What do you remember about Sophie? Why were you the one who brought her on the train to me? Were you sad when she left? I want to tell him how much that baby missed him, how she wailed and refused to sleep for weeks, how, despite her grief, she decided on the second day that I was hers and that no one else was leaving her again. From then on, she never let me out of her clutch. I wonder how to say all this, our different languages and cultures and experiences creating a dense forest, with few tools to carve a path.

But we manage to hack through a series of rudimentary questions and answers. The Man used to stop by the orphanage after work, and while he waited for his wife he played with the babies. Sophie preferred him to everyone else. Every day she waited for him to come. Soon he came especially to see her.

Grace is worn out from translating all of this, and the food starts to arrive. A waitress brings a platter of flat green vegetables the color of spinach. "All the dishes here are local," Grace says, searching for another word. "Organic."

"What's this?" I spoon some vegetables up for Sophie and me.

"Leaves from the trees," Grace says.

Another dish arrives, a heap of greens with the stringy appearance of cooked spinach. Spinach, it seems, has become my all-purpose reference point. "What's this?" I ask.

"Seaweed," Grace announces. We each scoop some up while Grace exchanges a few words with Mr. Feng. She turns back. "But not from the sea," she says. "From the mountain."

Oh, I think. Weeds.

A waitress places a platter of meat on our turntable, topped by two claw-like shapes.

"And that?" I ask.

"Chicken." Grace looks puzzled at my ignorance. But of course: those are the chicken's grizzled feet right there on top.

We try some weeds from the mountain and leaves from the trees and chicken and sweet and sour pork with the bones still in. Next comes fish head soup. The Man keeps an eye on Sophie's plate, refilling it regularly. She gamely eats whatever he gives her.

Grace chats with the others, occasionally passing tidbits of information on to me. Mr. Lu remembers bringing Sophie to Hangzhou on the train, she says.

Grace looks tired after four hours of walking in the heat and driving and translating. So I try to decide, just as I did 10 years ago, on just one question that will yield something meaningful for Sophie, who doesn't know what to ask either.

Ten years ago I had approximately 10 seconds to ask The Man a question. "What would he like me to tell her someday about him?" I asked.

She rolled her eyes at the sentimentality of adopting parents. Clearly reluctant, she addressed The Man, who answered briefly.

I wanted him to say that she was special to him, that he would always remember her, and that he hoped she would grow up smart and strong, some words of affection or wisdom.

The interpreter turned to me and said in a bored voice, "He says, thank you for adopting her."

Ten years later here I am again, searching for the one right question, looking for an answer that will assure my daughter of her enormous worth. But the sun and all the food have turned me sluggish or maybe just resigned, knowing that few of us ever really find any such question or answer. So when The Man says what I've been waiting to hear, it passes by in a blur, one leaf fluttering to the ground in a landscape of trees, one fleck of rice in the front hall, shaken off by a shoe, threatening to go by the wayside.

"When she left," Grace says to me, "he cried and cried."

"She was sad, too," I answer. "She missed him."

Waitresses clear our table and bring takeout containers.

"He says that Sophie is lucky to have a mother who brought her back," Grace says. "He says that you are both lucky."

I nod. We are.

I wish I could ask his wife more questions about working at the orphanage. I would like to know what The Man sells in his shop. I wish he knew that the baby he once played with makes good grades, and plays the clarinet, and does gymnastics, and loves dogs. What he knows is that she is happy and healthy. What we know is that when she left China, he cried and cried. We pile into the van and head through the clouds of dust we kick up to drop the Lus off at their construction site.

After we call out our goodbyes, promising to visit again, we head on down the highway, past haystacks sculpted like little huts and road workers in baseball caps and the occasional yellow hard hat. Sophie starts to nod off and I drowse, too, in the hot wind blowing through the van. Half-asleep, I imagine I am holding something, a souvenir of some sort, and then I jolt awake. My hands are empty, but they feel full, as if I now have something tangible, solid and three-dimensional to take home: The certainty that my child was loved before I met her. There's so much we will never know, but we know this, and for now that is enough.

Nancy McCabe is the author of three travel memoirs: "From Little Houses to Little Women: Revisiting A Literary Childhood," in which she rereads favorite children's books and visits sites and tourist attractions related to them; and two about adoption-related travel in China, "Crossing the Blue Willow Bridge: A Journey to My Daughter's Birthplace in China;" and "Meeting Sophie: A Memoir of Adoption." Her work has received a Pushcart Prize and appeared in many magazines and anthologies.

MILLION DOLLAR QUESTIONS
Cambodia

Cambodia feels like an open wound. Still raw from a scrape with death, still aching from its painful roots. Reminders of the genocide are everywhere: in the eerie absence of the elderly; in the mountains of garbage that clutter the roads and define the landscape; in the pleading tone of the desperate *tuk tuk* driver, hoping for a day of work; and in the perfectly rehearsed sales pitches of the children peddling baskets of discounted Lonely Planet guidebooks on every street corner.

For the second time in five months, I am walking the half-mile stretch to cross the border at Poipet — the gateway into Cambodia and the portal to its poverty. It's hotter this time. It's now summer, and the tropical sun rules the land in a brutal tyranny. After eight months of traveling, I've grown accustomed to the musty stench of my soiled clothes and the taxing load of my backpack that contains everything I own, but never to the heat.

As I walk under the stone archway inviting me into the Kingdom of Cambodia, the black dots of dehydration appear in my periphery like passing planets to a sun-bound astronaut who's drifted off course. My head is forever trapped in a fogged-up fishbowl.

Poipet is not a coastal town, yet everywhere there is evidence of a shipwreck. Scraps of plastic, cardboard, Styrofoam, metal and human flotsam appear to have washed ashore. The people I see seem like the only sur-vivors, still recovering from this thalassic catastrophe. Families huddle together under facades of crumbling concrete that once were homes. Everyone walks slowly, staring at nothing, myself among them. I can feel crow's feet forming in the corners of my eyes from all the squinting. One thought raps relentlessly on the front door of my frontal lobe: I need water.

I search in vain for someone who looks like they might be sitting on a cooler, a makeshift minimart that often flanks the streets. But for the first time in South-east Asia, I can't find anyone to sell me anything. People are preoccupied, squatting low, on their haunches, with their faces covered and averted from the sun, trying to avoid the heat.

I am jolted from my feverish quest by a tug on my pinky finger. Two deep, dark eyes stare up at me, their depths like the abyss of a cave. A girl who looks to be about 3 stands obstinately before me like an avant-garde performance art piece. The canvas of skin covering her bones appears painted in haste, with sloppy brushstrokes, muddy streaks. She clamps her entire hand around my littlest finger with a firm grip and without the slightest indication of letting go.

"Excuse me, lady, one dollar. I need a dollar, lady. Please, lady, give me a dollar," she chants.

I have a dollar. In fact, I have 300 of them stuffed neatly at the bottom of my pack. I had stashed them away for this very trip to Cambodia. As my semester teaching in Thailand neared its end, I carefully regulated every saved penny from my salary to fund a final trip around Southeast Asia before returning home to Atlanta.

Never give money to panhandling children; it perpetuates their livelihood as beggars, I repeat in my head, the way I used to prepare for lessons and study for tests.

I had spent weeks reading and researching everything from personal blogs to the BBC. And every source answered my question of whether to give money to child beggars with a firm and stern don't do it. They each echoed the same warning: "By feeling pity, giving money and food, child labor — a growing business — is supported and the children are sustained on the streets." On paper, it made sense. And my response seemed easy.

But standing face to face with a 3-year-old in Cambodia, my heart sinks and I panic. As a teacher and a student, I have never been as unsure of my answers. I can't stop myself from thinking: What if they are wrong?

Reluctant to pull my finger from hers, we walk pinky-in-hand for several more steps before I finally untangle myself from her taut grip. I look at her and she expects me to speak, but instead of answering her question or acknowledging her presence, I look away. Our locked eyes make me feel a thousand times heavier than the 50 pounds I am carrying. Eventually I tell her "No, I'm sorry," but she follows me, tries to walk in my path, demanding me to notice her. She repeats her haunting mantra as if in a trance, "Just a dollar, lady."

*****

Ten months before, I was in Atlanta, sitting on my bed, thumbing the glossy pages of a National Geographic and fantasizing about the day I would soon be in Cambodia. It was a picture of Ta Prohm that had summoned me. The 12th-century, tree-entwined Buddhist monastery was the stage for Lara Croft's adventures in "Tomb Raider" and is one of hundreds of ancient temples that stand alongside Angkor Wat in Siem Reap. On two full pages, creeping strangler figs and slinking lichens devoured the once-indestructible ruins. It was a perfect crystallization of nature's dominance over mankind, a reminder that nature can undermine even the apotheosis of human creations. I ripped out the pages and kept them in my purse for weeks. I wanted to be here, to feel small, and to stay inside this photograph forever.

When the day came for me to shrink my life into a backpack, I was staying at a friend's house. Scattered across her floor were the remainders of my purged possessions and the things I would take with me. There were stacks of clothes separated into two piles — one for teaching and one for adventuring. There were labeled Ziploc bags, a diary of Anaïs Nin, a Canon Rebel, plus an empty journal and a manila folder stuffed full of goodbye cards addressed "Dear Miss Josalin."

There were 50 of them, actually, one from every kid at SoulShine, the liberal afterschool program I worked at as a teacher and counselor in Atlanta. I picked up a card signed "Love, Emilia," depicting an underwater scene: blue, squiggly lines for waves, spider-like crabs, swaying palm trees and a mermaid replica, exactly the way I would have drawn it. For months at SoulShine there was a mermaid craze, and it all began with Emilia.

Every day after school she would rush inside, throw her backpack to the floor, scarf down a hasty snack, and climb onto my lap. I loved the way her crimson curls bounced, giving off warmth and complementing her fiery spirit. I would twirl them in my fingers and she would ask, without fail, "Miss Josalin, today can we draw mermaids?"

I am not an artist and my drawings were, at best, mediocre. But to Emilia, they were masterpieces. She praised me for them, begging me to teach her every step of my drawing process, eventually surpassing my talent and producing them en masse. The kids at SoulShine started to take notice, and soon every girl and even some boys were bombarding me with requests for drawing lessons. For hours after school, I would show them how two pencil strokes could make a ponytail and how a mix of blues, greens and gold glitter create an iridescent fin. How a "3" and a capital "E" formed the outlines of a seashell chemise, and how long eyelashes make the mermaid feminine.

Flipping through my cards, I saw dozens of mermaids. I closed the manila folder and wedged it alongside the few other carefully chosen items in my pack.

*****

In Poipet, I surrender my quest for water and opt for a beer instead. It's 10 in the morning, but I feel like I've been in this city for centuries, and the cold, foamy taste in my mouth provides a refreshing relief. I try to focus, envisioning Ta Prohm, and examining the bus schedule to Siem Reap. Waiting for the bus, a young girl races me to the trash can to salvage my beer can. She wears a ponytail and shuffles by with shaky, knobby knees, hunched over like an old woman. Her shiny, thick hair whips like the tail of a black stallion, with features both bold and refined, in utter defiance to her demeanor. She holds her T-shirt stretched out like a basket in which she carries her collection of tourists' trash — her treasures.

I watch her attempt to add my can to the pile and fail. Her shirt collapses, revealing her scrawny frame, and bottles and cans topple in every direction toward the ground. She looks around, eyes racing with the trajectory of launched pinballs. Gathering the bottles, she drops them two more times before scurrying away. In a few seconds, she vanishes from my sight, but her presence lingers in my mind. Sitting and waiting, I wonder: Would these children be forced to sell and beg and scrounge and steal for their lives if their families hadn't been butchered and uprooted in a ruthless genocide?

From 1975 to 1979, Cambodia's government systematically massacred three million of its own people. Promoting a radical agenda of nationwide ethnic cleansing, Pol Pot and his obedient Khmer Rouge regime rivaled the Nazis in organized cruelty. With horrifying gusto, their motive was to purge and reform the population in place of a pure, agrarian Communist society.

The entire country suffered, but the Khmer Rouge singled out certain people as the enemy. Among those targeted were intellectuals, city folks, minorities, teachers, writers, doctors and people who wore glasses. When the Khmer Rouge took power, it captured Phnom Penh, the capital, and evacuated the entire city in three days. Once-bustling, thriving cities became wastelands and torture camps. The displaced people met their fate in an orderly fashion: They were herded to labor camps, then torture prisons and, ultimately, to their death in the killing fields.

My bus pulls out of the station and leaves the forgotten shipwreck survivors to fend for themselves. Poipet disappears behind me in a dusty dirt cloud like the phantasmagoria of strange dreams. I gaze out the window at vast, barren fields and conical tops of straw hats and wonder what the people beneath them had seen and felt and suffered when Pol Pot reigned supreme.

To save cash and prevent scams, I rent a bike from my hostel in Siem Reap at dawn the next morning. After pedaling 10 kilometers of dirt roads and dodging tuk tuks, I am finally amid the ancient ruins of the Angkor Empire. It is low season, so there are not many tourists, most of them choosing to avoid the oppressive heat. Normally this would be a good thing, but in Cambodia it means I am an easy target.

I arrive at Ta Prohm temple with high expectations, burning thighs and half the vigor of Lara Croft. As at many of the popular Angkor temples, the atmosphere is frenzied. Tourists strike stupid poses, snap photos in rapid succession, and discover hidden crevices by way of their own routes. Local merchants cast their well-practiced lines into a sea of unsuspecting tourists and wait to see who falls for the bait. Their merchandise is often handmade: wood-carved finger flutes, jangly jewelry, charcoal sketches of Angkor Wat, and hand-painted clothing. All for $1.

Through the chaos and crowded amalgam of flashy new Apple products and sweaty bodies, I see my enchantress. The divine tree fatally intertwined with the ruins from the two-page photograph. Like a comfortable houseguest she sprawls out and makes herself at home in a sacred room of the ancient monastery.

I situate myself in just the right place and take the very same photograph, though not as high-res and with an amateur's eye. I take hundreds more as I explore Ta Prohm. It provides me with endless inspiration, and the ruins invoke my creative spirit. But what captivates me is a pair of young merchants. A brother and sister no older than 9 years old with bright red baskets and stock-brokers' enthusiasm. Squatting on a mound of rocks that have been squeezed out of place by thick, gnarled roots reclaiming the jungle, they scope out the torrent of tourists entering their domain. They wait like watchdogs, sniffing me out immediately.

"Lady, I have very nice jewelry for you. Come here, lady. I have many, many things for one dollar," the girl says, arms draped with bracelets from her wrists to her armpits.

I've prepared something to say this time. Silence, I convince myself, reveals weakness. I try to appear honest and confident, hoping my answers will suffice them.

"I can't today. I will be back though. I will come and buy some tomorrow."

She glares hard at me. Her brother stands behind her with one hand on his hip, the other cradling his basket like a baby. I shrug my shoulders and reveal my empty hands.

"Not tomorrow!" she says, now indignant and miffed by me. "You buy now, lady. Tomorrow, I do not see you." Wiping the palm of her hand down her face, "All farangs (foreigners) look the same."

And indeed she does not see me. She sees what she wants to see: a rich, white tourist crippled by guilt who might dish out pity in the form of American dollars. And I try hard, but I do not see her either. I want to see a 9-year-old who runs through the ruins playing hide-and-seek with her brother, laughing and skipping, and free to just be. I want her to hold my hand and ask me about my funny clothes or my pale skin or if she can braid my hair. I want to see a child with the innocence that reminds me not to take life too seriously.

Just then, the wind kicks a slight breeze. A delicate dandelion flower floats by, hovering in the air briefly. The two siblings fall silent and still, their eyes fixed on this evanescent wisp of beauty until it drifts out of sight. And in this moment, they abandon their roles as pushy street merchants and again become children. I snap a photo of their sudden transformation and steal this moment for myself. When the dandelion vanishes, so too does their laughter and wonder. In Cambodia, this phenomenon of children behaving like children surfaces only in glimpses. I take a few more unimportant shots of big trees and crumbling rocks and exit the temple.

To my surprise, my bike — secured with a flimsy, shoestring-sized cable lock — is right where I left it. I try to drone out the cacophony of auctioneers offering me water and make a beeline for my two-wheeled geta-way. But I am promptly intercepted and detained by a thin, young boy and eager guide. His hands are callused, and I feel tender when they touch me, grabbing my arm and dragging me along quickly. He seems like he has something to show me, but I soon realize it is me that he is showing.

He presents me to a group of kids of staggering heights and ages. They are his cohorts and his siblings, and it is clear who calls the shots. He points to the youngest, gives her the cue, and she yokes me with her eyes and begins rattling off her ABCs.

"She can say her ABCs for one dollar," my kidnapper says proudly.

I look around for an adult, but I see no one. And I remember reading that parents often get their children to do their begging for them. Smaller, cuter and livelier, they have been proven more successful on the streets.

When he sees me turning to walk away, he runs after me, trailed closely behind by his well-trained posse. They crowd around me, hurling English phrases and fragments, convinced of their ability to sway me.

"Look, I can count to 10! One, two, three, four....How about 10 bracelets for one dollar or a bottle of water? You are very thirsty, lady."

I had seen this business savvy before. The same pre-cocity, but with different motives.

*****

A master of the ocean realm, Emilia soon advanced to drawing castle-dwelling beauties. She was diligent and her hobby easily gained momentum within her circle of friends. She started a drawing club composed of six core members and a handful of transient contributors who came and went depending on the day. After snack, Emilia would dump out every box of crayons into a massive pile in the middle of them, and the others would elbow each other to get a spot at the big picnic table. First attempts at mermaids, princesses, dragons and castles littered the floor daily. Somehow crayon nubs covered entire pages with fantastic scenes and not an inch of wasted paper.

They drew constantly. And in a seamless transition from schoolgirl to sales executive, Emilia started a business.

"Miss Josalin, look at the mermaid I drew, just like you!" Emilia boasted. "Will you buy a picture?"

"Oh yeah? How much?" I asked, amused.

"You can get one for 50 cents or four for $1!"

Of course I bought them. I bought them all, with whatever change I had lying at the bottom of my purse. It didn't seem to make a difference if I gave a dollar to some children. But these were children who had three meals a day and shoes on their feet. Children who got back rubs for bad dreams, and Band-Aids for boo-boos, and kisses just because. They didn't need my money. The quarters I gave them would gather dust at the bottom of their piggybanks.

In Cambodia, my dollar holds power. And I'm unsure of how to wield it. Sometimes, I think I came here expecting to watch a performance, like an audience member snug and relaxed in her seat. Instead, with the swift crossing of the border, I am dragged on stage and thrust into the scene. How am I supposed to act? What am I supposed to say? The plot is complex, and no one gave me a script. Uncomfortable and blinded by the spotlight, I improvise. I hold my breath, believing that a botched line or a missed cue could sabotage the entire show.

I am constantly torn, thoughts bisected between not knowing how to help and how not to hurt. I struggle to reconcile my heart with my head, my guilt with my gut, constantly. I am suspended in a state of hopelessness and inner conflict, always. Here, I am forced to confront life's injustices and contradictions. Here, I learn that there is not an answer for everything. The aftermath of genocide is not easily reversed, and the people will go on suffering, creating, destroying, and ever enduring.

Josalin Saffer lays her roots in Atlanta, GA, where she received a B.A. degree in journalism. In 2012, she spent her first year abroad living, writing and working as an English teacher in Thailand and exploring Southeast

Asia. Now, she is continuing her journey as a writer and teacher in the Czech Republic. Her writing has appeared in The Guardian Weekly, the Matador Network and South East Asia Backpacker magazine. To read more of her published work, visit www.josalinsaffer.com.

TUMBLEWEED
Around the World

"You can't keep me down on the farm," I joked to my future husband.

"Huh? What farm?" he asked.

We were sitting in a busy New Haven restaurant. Nearby was the Yale Art Gallery, the Schubert Theater, the hustle of traffic on Chapel Street.

There were no farms visible.

"I mean, I'm a born traveler," I said. "I measure everything in frequent flyer miles."

"Oh?" he said, looking wary.

"Is there something wrong?" I asked.

"I'm afraid I'm a stay-at-home kind of guy," Douglas said softly. "I used to travel, but now I have health issues. Airplanes are a problem."

"That's OK. I'm happy going off by myself."

"Alone?" he asked.

"Actually, I prefer to travel alone."

Douglas looked at me in surprise.

"I've never known anyone like you," he said.

"Well, now you do," I said with a laugh and more than a hint of feistiness.

The next week I left for a month in Mexico.

Douglas and I had met and fallen in love at a good point in our lives. We were what you'd call "mature." We'd each been married before and our children were grown. Although we had many values in common, we also had wide disparities in our tastes, lifestyle and personalities. Fortunately, we were old enough to revel in them.

He soon started calling me "Tumbleweed."

In the 15 years we've been together I've taken off for China, Mongolia, Mexico, Costa Rica, Japan, California, the Pacific Northwest, Canada, the Caribbean and India. I've walked alone from France to Spain on the Camino de Santiago and I've trekked almost 1,400 kilometers (about 870 miles) around the island of Shikoku in Japan.

Meanwhile, Douglas stays back in the quiet, familiar suburbs of Connecticut. He has work, family, friends and activities that satisfy him. I have a flexible career and a well-worn passport.

Most important, our marriage remains healthy and intact.

I find myself frequently encouraging other women to hit the road, or the friendly skies, or even the choppy waters of a Windjammer by themselves. Whether they are married or not, partnered or not. Whether they are young or old.

Solo travel has its own rewards which duo travel can't match.

When two or more people travel together they tend to create a private bubble. Whether they are walking, dining or sightseeing, they often focus on each other. Their reactions impact each other. At the very least they are constantly aware of each other's needs and wishes.

"I'm hungry" says one.

"I don't want to eat yet," says the other.

Compromise is an understood part of the package. Partnered travel is a two-way street.

Single travel is more of a boulevard or a round-about, sometimes an alley or a cul-de-sac. You just never know.

When I travel alone, my eyes are focused outward. Who and what is around me? I give out smiles and receive smiles in return. I observe and take note. I eavesdrop like a nosy neighbor,

I welcome the chance encounter, the curious glance of the child, the friendly shopkeeper, the person willing to give me directions or share her city. I practice languages and pick up words in new ones.

Once, on a whim, I took a night bus (cheap!) from Santiago to Bilbao, Spain. Who wouldn't want to see the marvels of the Bilbao Guggenheim Museum? But upon arrival, in the early, foggy, hours of the morning, I realized that the bus stop did not seem to be anywhere near the center of town. I wondered which misty route to follow. The one tumbled-down taxi stand was empty, the information booth shuttered with a metal eyelid. Then a fellow passenger, an older woman who had sat behind me on the bus, noticed that I was standing off to the side, shifting my backpack and looking perplexed.

She said something in Basque. I responded in Spanish.

"This is my city," she said, switching tongues. "Where do you want to go?"

"The museum," I answered, "but I suppose it's way too early."

"Yes, way too early, but it's a beautiful morning for a foggy walk," she said. "You've obviously just hiked the Camino de Santiago," she said. "I saw the traditional scallop shell dangling off your backpack when you got on."

"Yes," I said, thinking she could probably also detect the ripe odor of my well-worn hiking boots.

"I'll lead you on foot to the center of Bilbao," she said. "It's a few kilometers."

I quickly looked her over and made a snap judgment. Her manner was frank, but pleasant. She was neither well-dressed nor poorly dressed. She was articulate, but speaking slowly, aware of my foreigner's Spanish. She had a book under one arm and a small bag.

The book sold me. At least this was a person who read. She was bound to be interesting.

I accepted her offer with gratitude.

We walked and walked, at one point stopping to rest in a city park where workers were sweeping up the trash from a festival that had taken place the night before. Every once in a while, I caught a whiff of garden soil and the scent of the distant sea.

She produced an orange from her bag and handed me a few plump slices. I offered biscuits and dried fruit. A shared breakfast.

She told me about the pain of growing up as a child under Franco, confessing her love for the Basque language, once forbidden. She pointed out landmarks in the slowly lifting fog.

There was something almost conspiratorial about our conversation. We talked about being wives, raising children, the deaths of our parents, our work and our frustrations. Through her eyes, I got to see Bilbao waking up, stretching and starting its day.

Would she have helped a group of travelers? Probably not. Most people consider groups to be self-sufficient. Would she have come to the aid of a couple? Maybe. But I like to think that she identified with my solitude.

I think the secret to successful solo traveling is to cultivate an open attitude. Not naive, not gullible, but welcoming to others. It's the opposite of the "Do Not Disturb" sign on a hotel door. As a woman traveling alone, I want someone to knock on my door, so to speak. Not literally, but emotionally and socially. Whether I am on a train or in a restaurant, I welcome people asking me where I'm from, striking up a conversation and sharing a piece of themselves with me.

And I want to knock on the doors of others.

I don't hesitate to initiate conversations.

Am I rebuffed? Sometimes.

Am I discouraged if I get no response? Not at all.

If someone ignores me or snarls or gives me an eye-roll, I just figure that there will be a friendlier person in the next town. Or maybe in the next 5 minutes.

Of course, I need to convey just the right amount of accessibility so that others engage with me in positive ways.

And obviously, social connection is easier in some cultures than others.

Once, on a voyage to Manuel Antonio National Park in Costa Rica, I had placed my bag on the beach while I dipped my toes in the Pacific. A capuchin monkey had rifled through my belongings and strewn them along the sand. As I was picking up sunglasses and sandals, I smiled at a young couple passing by. They laughed at the situation. The silly tourista who left bananas in her bag. They stopped to help me get my possessions away from the determined creature. Nuria and Juan were local "ticos" enjoying the national park. We got to talking. Their friendliness, combined with a laid-back Costa Rican sense of time, meant that we wouldn't part company for another few hours. We hiked together all morning. Then they introduced me to a friend who rented kayaks after I had expressed my interest in a short paddle on the Damas River.

I bumped into them later as I was returning to my hotel.

"Josimar says you flipped over!" said Juan.

The embarrassing news had already reached their ears.

"And he says you lost your sun hat," added Nuria. "It floated away!"

We chatted for a while like old friends. The day ended with my being invited to Nuria's mother's house for a supper of beans, rice and fresh dorado.

We solo female travelers often take pride in our independence. But too much independence can limit our social interactions. I find that asking for suggestions, getting help, accepting invitations and leaning a bit on others is a critical part of traveling solo successfully.

While in India on a visit to Varanasi, I got it into my head that I would ride a horse along the Ganges River. From my hotel, at the top of one of the main bathing ghats, I could see the wide sandy flats on the other side and distant figures of horseback riders. I waited until the locals had finished their morning ablutions to hire a rowboat. I was determined to feel the wind in my hair and the reins in my hands.

Fortunately, on my way down from the hotel, I traded smiles with a delightful couple, Sunil and Hetal, who were sitting on a bench waiting for relatives who had gone to the Hindu temple. Both families were on holiday from Delhi.

I decided to ask for advice.

"Yes, of course it's possible to rent a boat to take you over there, but you must agree on the round-trip price beforehand and make sure the boatman waits for you," cautioned Sunil.

"Otherwise, no one will bring you back unless you pay 2,000 rupees. Or more!" added Hetal.

I hadn't thought of that. I assumed the rowboats went back and forth easily like taxis.

"Like taxis, yes," said Sunil, "but they will see you're stuck and will take advantage of the situation."

I nodded.

"I'm sorry, that's just the way it is," he said in his lilting English, smiling at me with a full set of teeth the color of piano keys.

We talked about Indian bargaining, the Varanasi touts, and the pleasures of buffalo milk ice cream.

Hetal, for her part, had a ton of direct questions for me. My nationality, my age and my reasons for being in India.

Primarily, she wanted to know if I had a husband.

I struggled to explain my situation.

"So your husband is home doing laundry and getting his own meals," she asked, "while you are here trying to ride a horse?"

"That's true," I said.

I didn't expect Hetal to really comprehend my life-style.

Even American friends back home sometimes shake their heads.

"Doesn't it get lonely, traveling by yourself?" people will ask.

"I guess it helps if you like your own company," I answer. "And if you have an outgoing personality."

The truth is that I'm not self-conscious eating alone in a restaurant or walking down the street or checking into a hotel. The world is full of people just like me. I don't think of my "singleness" as an anomaly.

"Who do you talk to?" some people ask.

For me, one of the pleasures of travel is learning and practicing foreign languages. I know five or six well enough to function. But there are plenty of places I travel where I can barely mutter "Please" or "Thank You" in the local lingo. Yet I always find ways to communicate.

Once I took an 18-hour train ride in China from the southern provinces into Beijing. Since I can't spit out more than a few words of Mandarin, I knew I would need to rely on my wits and universal gestures if I were going to have any social interactions. With a little luck, by the time the trip was over I had played cards with strangers, given a few English lessons, learned a song in Cantonese, and exchanged snacks with seat mates. Upon arrival, I was exhausted, but far from lonely.

"Well, you could have read a book," said a friend when I told her about the experience on the Chinese train.

"But if I had been reading, that would have changed everything."

Sometimes I see a solo woman traveler with her nose in her journal or a novel or a tablet. I wonder why. Yes, sometimes one needs and welcomes a quiet, reflective space, but all too often the reading/writing traveler is merely erecting a barrier between herself and others. Perhaps she is feeling awkward occupying just one seat at a table meant for two. But her book or phone keeps others at bay, as if she is saying, "Leave me alone. I'm deeply engrossed in Barbara Kingsolver or Haruki Murakami or opening up an email from my insurance company."

It's often better to just sit peacefully alert. Make small talk with the waiter, or savor your food.

Keep the "Please Disturb" sign in an obvious place around your neck.

That's why I like to frequent restaurants during the off-peak hours when the wait staff isn't frantic and the locals are no longer jostling each other for a precious table. Often, when I am in Paris, I go to a popular crêpe shop in the 6th arrondissement as soon as the lunch crowd begins to thin out. Even the owner has time to talk to me about his source for *sarrasin* (a certain flour.) He offers me some cider on the house. It helps that I speak French, of course, but none of this pleasant contact would happen if I kept my head buried in the headlines of Le Monde, or my eyes glued to my iPhone screen.

Of course, people often ask about my sense of safety.

"Aren't you afraid, all by your lonesome?"

I don't put myself purposely into dicey situations. I'm not looking for drugs or contraband or a one-night stand. I'm always aware of my surroundings. But that's just street smarts. For anyone. Male or female. At home or abroad.

I think that the trick for solo female travelers is to balance self-protection with healthy risk. Life is risk. If we don't stick our big toe or our leg into the water, we'll never get bitten by a shark or dragged by the undertow. But we won't find a starfish either. One has to learn to assess danger, read signs, and behave accordingly. I'm not hesitant to change train or bus seats if the "vibe" is wrong. I'm not afraid to venture down unknown streets, but I'm wise enough to reverse my direction if I'm being followed.

Just common sense.

As a solo traveler, I am often asked if I miss having someone to share my experiences with. Of course, there are moments when it might be nice to lean into the arms of my mate as the sun sinks like a stone into the canals of Amsterdam. But it's also exciting to come home to a warm welcome, with stories to tell and photos to share.

"I can't wait to see you!" texts the husband, like a new lover. "I can't wait to see you, too," I write back.

Sometimes he's bought fresh flowers.

Whenever I have a perfect travel moment — a vista or a meal or an encounter — I just try to absorb the good feelings. Really absorb them. With all my senses. Breathe in the moment, like the bouquet of a fine wine.

How lucky I am to work and travel the world, to enjoy other cultures and customs. Taking in a beautiful sunset, whether shared or not, contributes to my well-being. So does traipsing through the cloud forest of Monteverde or eating the first asparagus of the season at the Beelitzer Spargelfest. It's all good, in and of itself. It can't be bottled or exported, just internalized.

Travel makes me happy. Uncovering new faces and places gives me tremendous satisfaction. It links me to the rhythms of life itself. It shapes my spirit, and by extension, it molds my marriage. When I return to the steady habits of Connecticut, I come back with a renewed zest for living and a deep appreciation of home.

Gabriella Brand says she was born with a backpack and a passport. Her fiction, essays and poetry have appeared in Room Magazine, StepAway, The Binnacle, The First Line, The Christian Science Monitor and several anthologies. She was a contributor to the Chance Encounters anthology published by World Traveler Press in 2014. One of her short stories was nominated for a Pushcart Prize in 2013. She lives in Connecticut, where she teaches foreign languages.

GIVING THANKS AT PULEMELEI
Samoa

"Are you going far?" the Samoan man asked as he leaned into my creaky rental car. We were under the shade of a dusty avocado tree. His bulk filled the entire space of my open window.

When he'd flagged me down, I'd thought he was an elder collecting a "customs fee," the few dollars it costs to use village roads that lead to many of Samoa's sights. He had been sitting idly in a greying roadside shack built for such occasions, but he wasn't asking for money, he was trying to hitch a ride.

I didn't want to pick him up, but I'd already stopped and I needed directions.

"I'm trying to get to Pulemelei Mound," I said, trying not to sound as lost as I was. "Do you know how to get there?"

"Mmm," he said raising his eyebrows in the classic Polynesian gesture for yes. "I need to pick up my car at the mechanic, but no hurry. I'll take you there first if you want."

Normally I wouldn't pick up a hitchhiker, especially not such a huge one, but this man had such a gentle expression that I sensed he was OK. Having spent 15 years of my life in and around Tahiti, which has a similar culture, I knew Polynesians pretty well — hulks with the temperament of bunny rabbits are common. Plus, if he knew where Pulemelei Mound was, I had just gotten closer to a dream. Over the past few days I'd narrowed down the ancient site's location to be near this village, but no one seemed to know exactly how to get there.

I had wanted to go to Pulemelei Mound since I'd heard it mentioned in an archaeology class years ago, but now that I was here in Samoa, I was having a hell of a time finding it. The "mound" is actually a pyramid 40 feet high, and 197 by 213 feet at its base — a little more than one-third the height of Kukulkan pyramid in Chichen Itza, Mexico, and slightly wider. Like many of the world's pyramids, Pulemelei is oriented to the cardinal directions. It was built around 1300 (probably a few hundred years after Kukulkan), and no one knows what it was used for. But one thing is certain: It's the largest ancient structure in Polynesia.

You'd think that a giant pyramid in the heart of Polynesia would be a major sight or at least something that a lot of people had heard of, but it isn't. The mound lies on a weed-ridden plot of disputed land, eaten by jungle, and few people know where it is.

My accidental hitchhiker's affirmative raise of the eyebrows was the most promising prospect I'd had in a week.

"Hop in," I told him.

We rattled along the road in silence for a few minutes. Half a dozen chickens squawked off to the side as we passed, escaping into a hibiscus hedge next to a house painted orange and blue. The hot air through our open windows mixed with a hint of smoke from burning leaves and the sweet scent of flowers. Faintly, in the distance, I could hear women's laughter.

Then, my new friend broke the silence and, simultaneously, my hopes.

"I've never been to Pulemelei," he said as we bumped over a particularly big pothole. "It's funny, I've lived here almost a year but I never thought of going."

His arm hung limply out the open passenger seat window and he gazed with a half-smile toward the bleached grey road in front of us. Every muscle in my body dropped in disappointment.

"Damn," I thought. Not only did he probably not know how to get there, he wasn't even a real local.

"Where are you from then?" I asked, trying to sound upbeat.

"I lived in New Zealand for over 30 years," he said. "But I grew up in Apia."

Apia is the capital of Samoa, so he was a city kid, not the earth-under-his-feet farmer I had assumed. The 30 years in New Zealand explained his fantastic English.

"Ah," he said. "It's here to the right."

He pointed with his thumb toward an unmarked track. As I maneuvered the car onto the narrow, rocky trail, he sat leaning forward in his seat like an eager kid.

We bumped over the rough road bordered by low, dry weeds till it disappeared into a skinny path that lead to a clear, calf-deep stream. The air was a soft, dusty yellow. We parked and got out, then followed the path, wading across the narrow strip of cold water flowing over well-rounded volcanic rocks. A broader trail started on the other side.

Shortly beyond the river, the terrain turned into sturdy and sharp waist-high grass. The air was thick and smelled of wet plants. As we picked our way through the brush, my friend began telling me a bit about himself. He was the youth group leader at the Mormon Church and was taking a bunch of local kids on a hike up the island's tallest mountain the next day.

"Maybe I can bring them here too one day if we find it," he said hopefully.

A fallen rotted tree blocked our path, and we tucked under broken branches and found our way through brambles. We kept walking. I guessed we'd been trekking half a mile when I looked up and saw that my companion's face was covered in sweat droplets. I stopped to take a sip of water from my bottle and offered him some. He politely took a small gulp.

As we walked on I was beginning to feel very skeptical. It was hot, I hadn't brought enough water for two people and the trail was becoming more and more faint. Then, just as I was thinking of suggesting that we turn around, we came into a flat, open area of tall, lush grass surrounded by mango trees. The air turned from sour to fresh.

A faded sign was nailed to one of the trees and I could just make out the word "Parking." Yes, at one time, maybe 10 or more years ago and before the land disputes began (apparently between a foreign company and a local family), this road had been made for vehicles. People could simply drive here.

Wading through cool, soft grass another few hundred feet, we came to another board on a tree that was nearly engulfed by skinny yellow vines. There, barely visible, were the words: "Pulemelei Mound 150m."

We'd found it! In the hot shade it barely seemed real.

The sign marked a dark tunnel of jungle that, at first glance, looked more like a wall of weeds and vines than a pathway. But when we hunched down, it was indeed a passageway and we slowly and carefully began to walk through. Right away I realized the thick vines were climbing on the mound and we actually were walking upward on the mound itself. A minute later, the path opened to rays of sunshine, and the top of the mound was visible. We clambered over a dense patchwork of ferns and sticky lianas, over rounded stones and moss. And then, magic. We were standing on top of a Polynesian pyramid.

It wasn't pointy, like some pyramids, and the top was more of basketball court-sized plateau. In the sunshine the vegetation had bald patches revealing cantaloupe-sized, ancient brown stones. Below the mound was a thick mass of yellow-green coconut palms that descended a slight slope, and beyond that was a faraway blue-grey sea. Two stubby mango trees grew out of some pushed up stones to one side and the rest of the plateau was covered in purple flowers and swarms of blue and brown butterflies. It made me want to frolic and chase the butterflies. So that's exactly what I did. I felt like a 10-year-old Indiana Jones.

My friend wasn't fazed by my childish behavior and immediately went to pick a few ripe mangos. He sat under the trees and ate the fruit while gazing off over the coconut forest and the far-away sea with a look of contentment. When I got tired of running around in the heat, I sat with him in the shade and he offered me a mango. Sweet, sticky orange juice ran over my fingers. Life was delicious.

After about half an hour I remembered I had a ferry to catch. As reluctant as I was, we had to leave. I signaled to my companion and we got up from our shady seats and made our way to the edge of the top of the mound. He walked in front and I followed closely behind.

Then, just as we were about to descend, he stopped, turned toward me and placed his big Samoan hands on my shoulders. We were face to face and I could feel the damp heat of his hands through my T-shirt as I looked into his creased, smiling eyes. In the most natural and subtle way, he leaned down and kissed me gently on the cheek.

"Thank you," he said.

I knew that the cheek kiss is a common form of greeting and platonic affection in Samoan culture. But his gesture, however sweet, made me acutely aware that I was by myself in the jungle with a large man I'd just picked up hitchhiking. The adventure had at once become deeper and lost its dreamy air of perfection. I wanted simultaneously to hug him to let him know I felt grateful I was to be here too, and to get back to the car as quickly as possible.

We hiked down without talking. I sensed my companion had noticed that the cheek kiss changed our dynamic, but perhaps, like me, he wasn't completely sure how or why. In a fog of cultural confusion, we got in the car silently, then trundled back out to the main road and found the spot where he needed to be dropped off.

When we were almost there, he said, "You know, I could use a little help paying for my car."

I'd thought he might ask for money; people often do in Samoa. But it still hurt a little. He'd spent a few hours with me and I had been happy for his company. I felt stung by the way the experience had suddenly become yet another monetary transaction, but I honestly wanted to help this man out. He had gotten somewhere I thought I'd never find and had been lovely company along the way.

"How much do you need?" I asked.

He looked at me blankly. This wasn't something he could answer.

I handed him a 50 tala note, the equivalent of about $17. It was probably too much but despite the awkwardness following the kiss, I wanted to thank this man for helping me achieve a dream. Paying him didn't taint anything in the Polynesian sense, I knew. I had money and he didn't so it was normal and polite for me to be generous with him as he had been with his time. I'd just have to get over it. I'd had a pretty phenomenal day.

We looked each other in the eye once more before he left, in what I hope was wordless understanding. My friend looked happy — happy for the help paying for his car, happy to have discovered a special place and perhaps happy to have spent the day with a pleasant person from faraway. And this made me think: Even though we never asked each other's names, our serendipitous trip together to a place lost and sacred would be with both of us forever.

As he walked away I thought, Thank you, hoping that somehow he'd hear me. In my mind, I stopped him before he disappeared. Then I imagined that I put my small hands up on his massive shoulders, stretched up on tippy toes and kissed him sweetly on the cheek.

Celeste Brash spent 15 years in French Polynesia before recently moving to Portland, OR. She's contributed to more than 50 titles for Lonely Planet and has written for publications ranging from BBC Travel to Islands magazine. Her travels, often with her family, have taken her around the world, but her heart is stuck on the never-ending variety of islands in the South Pacific. She's writing a memoir about her five years living and raising her children on a remote black pearl farm.

THE MEMORY PALATE
France

At the open market, Francis Compte chooses *ecornet* (squid), our first course, two chickens, our main course. He passes yellow and zucchini under his finger pads, his hands moving quickly, weighing, bagging, and counting out change. Our evening meal begins at the open market, and I try to see as Francis sees, a strawberry's red ripeness, tomatoes without blemishes.

Before arriving in Auvillar, a village in southwestern France, I'd been encouraged to involve myself with the culture, perhaps picking grapes or cooking with a French chef. I love food; I love kitchens. So here I am shopping with Francis, chef and owner of Le Petit Palais. He looks into his woven basket and moves his lips, without speaking. Then, suddenly, as if remembering, he reaches for a box of raspberries. He angles his head. "*Ça va?*"

"*Ça Va.*" OK.

After spending 30 years in the States managing up-scale dining rooms (the Ritz in Chicago, a country club in Arizona), Francis has returned to his home country. Driving, now, with one hand, he sweeps an arm. "It is God's country, here, when it comes to fruits. The people? They haven't changed since I left. These farmers, they're complaining all the time, but they're pretty wealthy. Not so the small towns. There, things are not so good. Here, Sandell, let me show you."

He veers left and we climb into a medieval village. Storefronts are mostly empty, and I think of small Midwestern towns I visited driving west from Maine to Colorado. Commerce had left those towns, too. "See. There, Sandell. Are you looking? Once in this town there were two markets, two bistros, two hairdressers. See what's left? One hairdresser, and there only the cats go in."

We laugh, but he has made his point. Like Americans, the French are shopping in big-box stores. And the next step? I don't want to imagine agri-business here, but consolidation is happening. Driving out of the village, Francis slows the car. Small trees. Not apple. Not peach. "You see them, Sandell? Kiwi."

I don't. I do. Green fruit, hanging nearly invisibly. I like this man fate has set down in my path, a man who shows me, not only kiwi, but a glimpse of France's underside.

*****

That evening inside the kitchen of Le Petit Palais, Francis holds his elbows close to his sides and wields a wide-bladed knife, slicing carrots. His arm is muscled and strong, fingers supple. He wears a black T-shirt, black and white pin-striped trousers, a chef's apron tied at his waist. A Rolex sits prominently on his left wrist. I turn the bracelet of my Rolex, a gift from Dick, my husband, a man who these days prefers the living room couch to travel, yet waits patiently for my return. Francis points with his knife, and the hairs on our arms graze. Quickly, we step apart. Ever since I rode with him early that morning, something has sparked between us. I look down at my fingers, my wedding ring. Francis looks into the pot where he has dropped the carrots. "These we will boil, but not too long."

Above the stove, a shelf holds jars. In one a golden liquid. Chicken fat? My Polish-Russian Jewish, immigrant grandmother used to render fat from chickens, and it is as if she is here, the feather brush of her presence as time rolls back. I am 3, 4, 5 years old, standing on a wooden chair watching a fry pan where, inside, chicken skin turns to *griven*, crisp leavings. We all lived together then, my grandmother, my grandfather, my mother, my father and I in a yellow stucco house in Morristown, NJ. Speaking Yiddish, my grandmother tells me to stand back as she spoons up a single hot crisp. When the piece is cool enough, she feeds me with her fingers. I am my grandmother's constant companion, watching as she cleaves chickens as Francis cleaves, cutting away wing tips and back bones, scraping tissue with his fingers, holding up the bloody mess. "See how fresh. Sandell, do you see?"

The smell of raw meat turns Francis' hand into my grandmother's hand, her short thick fingers reaching for mine as we climb a hill into town, taking turns pulling my red wagon. At the chicken store, my grandmother pokes a finger into a wooden cage and presses into a chicken's breast to see if it is plump. At home, my grandmother removes the last of the pin feathers. She sets a pot on the stove and boils the chicken, feet and all.

Perhaps my love for my grandmother translated into my love for kitchens and for food, not only eating and preparing, but growing vegetables in my garden — pea pods, carrots and Brussels sprouts I wash, drizzle with olive oil, sprinkle with sea salt and roast with rosemary. Food conjures memory, the burnt scent of anger, the warm sip of comfort, the sweet taste of love. To know that Francis has chosen these chickens at the market, that he has hacked off necks and heads, that the zucchini he slices has passed from and beneath his appraising fingers enchants me. "Slicing," Francis says, "is about the knife."

I observe his knuckles, relaxed on the handle, blade moving as if hinged, rhythmically and, seemingly, effortlessly. Despite his calm, the air is electric. A flirtation, here, in a kitchen, my place of protection and love. Is this strange or strangely fitting?

"You can slice garlic the way you slice onion," Francis says, "but with garlic it's very important to get the stem out. It's bitter."

Just then, Francis' wife Jo appears in the doorway. She holds a fistful of forks and speaks in rapid French. Jo is a sturdy woman with long, waving red hair. "Sandell, do you want to eat inside or outside?" Francis says to me.

En plein air, where artists paint, setting up easels at the edges' fields or on the banks of the Garonne, a lazy river that flows past my studio window.

"Outside," I say.

Jo purses her lips, and I understand that serving inside is easier.

Our guests will be two writers, a sculptor, a photographer and a painter, all in residence at Moulin à Nef, an artists' colony where I, too, am staying. I smile, politely, but I have decided.

As Jo leaves, Francis stage-whispers. "She's jealous."

Are we obvious? Apparently so. A youthfulness has filled my body, not desire, not passion, but a feeling that if not thwarted could move in that direction. I will not let it. Nor will Francis. Yet, another day at another dinner, Francis will point and say, "If I was Muslim, I would marry Sandell, too."

Curling the fingers of my left hand over a large garlic clove and using the knuckle of my middle finger to guide a knife blade, I try to slice as Francis slices, rhythmically and surely. Head bowed, I steal a sideways glance at my teacher. He nods, approvingly. I ease my grip, and the knife grows lighter. Again, my grandmother is here, her hand guiding mine. Tactile in the kitchen, my grandmother grabs a handful of sliced apples, a lesser amount of raisins. I chop walnuts in her *shteisel*, a brass mortar and pestle, her kitchen my refuge. Here, the air does not hold the residue of my father's anger and his rage. My grandmother is the one my father does not cow. She wards him off with her wooden spoon. "*Gay avek.*" Go away. "*Meshugena.*" Crazy.

Alone with my grandmother, I breathe the rich aroma of chicken soup, the scent of *bupka*, yeast cake baking with cinnamon and sugar. "Taste," my grandmother says. "It's all right? You like it?"

I lift my knife. "You know, I used to be my grandmother's taster," I say to Francis.

The creases at his eyes crinkle. "Ah, no wonder you have come into my kitchen."

Kitchen as refuge. Kitchen as comfort, the meditation of repetitive movement like petting a dog or stroking a cat. Kitchen as love, the place where I prepare meals, Thanksgiving dinners, Passover Seders, winter stews. Summers, I cook with my granddaughters, steaming fresh picked beans, sprinkling olive oil, salt and pepper. I add cherry tomatoes and feta. Sitting outside on the deck, we mop up oil with crusty baguette.

Francis tosses a pinch of ginger into a dice of avocado, onion, cucumber and tomato, along with a smidgen of garlic. He is making Sauce Vierge. "I do not have the cilantro," Francis says, "so we'll do without the cilantro, for now."

At home in Maine, I no longer have cilantro, either. I planted early, and before I left for France all of my cilantro went to flower. But I believe cilantro will appear, magically, in this kitchen along with a bowl of my grandmother's chicken soup.

"Important, *sel* and pepper," Francis says, pinching from two small bowls. He squeezes the juice of half a lime and pours olive oil. His voice goes dreamy, and I understand he is speaking as much to himself as to me. "If I have some cilantro will be…" Alert to my presence, his voice brightens. "You serve this on chicken breast grilled. Want to try?"

I take up a spoon to eat one of my favorite tastes, gazpacho in dice.

Behind his glasses Francis' gray eyes flash. "As they say in America, that ain't bad."

He prepares a simple salad of celery root, that pale knobby underground vegetable, and tells me how to make a similar salad with fennel. "Lemon is e*mphatique*, so it doesn't get dark."

Emphatique? Ah, necessary.

Now, taking a jar from the refrigerator, he holds it aloft, giving me a boyish smile. "The French do such a good mayonnaise, I buy it." He offers a taste, and as I take the slaw from a spoon, I feel that potency between us. The slaw is savory, not too tart. Unmistakably, celery root — earthy, pungent.

Moving as if someone has upped his tempo, Francis places the halves of a single white fig into a pan of simmering Madeira and brown sugar. He squeezes a stream of lemon juice. Now, butter. As the fig cooks in its fragrant sauce, Francis prepares strawberries, spooning brown sugar, adding lime juice and ginger. He is in that place where thought gives way to the thing itself, a dancer's leap, a perfect throw. He mashes green peppercorns, then drops a pinch into the mix. Who would have thought, pepper and strawberries? He leans close. "This is for you and me."

I slip the bowl of the spoon into my mouth where flavors billow, tastes of sweet and sharp, sugar and pepper, the bite of ginger, then intense ripeness — those sun-warmed strawberries. With the same intensity he brings to his cooking, Francis watches my face. "Delicious," I say, lowering the spoon. Ah, this energy between us — like the taste of strawberry and pepper, an unexpected delight.

Again, Jo appears. "*Ça va?*"

"*Ça va,*" Francis says.

"*Ça va,*" I repeat.

"Bien," she says.

With the back of my hand, I brush a lock of hair from my forehead.

In an alcove, Jo takes a white cloth from a bureau, then walks to the front of the restaurant, her footsteps a silent echo on the wooden floor. It is as if I can see her spreading a white cloth on the outdoor table, then smoothing it with her long fingers. My friends will be our only guests. Francis has closed Le Petit Palais to cook with me. He transfers the single white fig to a bowl, adds butter, then, lifting the pan high, he swirls. He turns off the heat, sets the pan down, adds cream. Wrist loose, wire whisk spinning, he stirs. "Voila," he exclaims, lifting the pan one last time. A slow pour as liquid covers the resting fig. He offers a bowl. Aromas of butter and cream along with sweet Madeira waft upward. I take up fig and liquid. "Ummmm."

A slight pucker of his lips. "Maybe I should give cooking lessons. What do you think?"

He knows what I think. "Absolutely."

With his fingers, Francis tosses simple greens with olive oil, salt and pepper, then mounds them onto plates. He centers a large piece of grilled squid, scatters shrimp and curls of squid at the sides, and on the rim of each plate a sprinkling of peeled, seeded diced tomato. What the French call *le montage*. In English, the presentation. In either language, an expression of love and pleasure. I adore the beauty of food, color and shape, and the nearly magical transformation of raw to cooked, of whole to diced. Francis and I serve our guests. Jo pours wine. Francis insists I sit in the one remaining chair. I'd rather join him in the kitchen. "When you are finished," he says.

We lift our glasses to toast Francis. My friends toast me. I demur. Francis is the chef, not I.

Back in the kitchen, I see that Francis is spooning sauce for the main course onto plates. It is a rich sauce made with Madeira, chicken and beef stocks, cream and *cepes*, porcini mushrooms. He tops each pool with a drumstick and a chunk of breast meat. "Everyone, Sandell, will have a sampling of dark meat and light." He arranges matchstick slices of sautéed yellow and green squash. Did he sauté with duck fat? That was the golden liquid — duck fat, not chicken. One by one, he stacks green beans. He lifts a basket from a fryer then, with bare fingers, he quickly removes each small potato. "Even a simple chicken you can make it special," he says with a grin.

On *shabbos* my grandmother serves slices of boiled chicken with freshly grated horseradish she mixes with vinegar and sugar. She bakes a potato kugel — grated potato mixed with beaten egg, salt, pepper, a pinch of flour — until it is crisp on the outside and soft on the inside. She slices carrots into pennies, boils, drains, sweetens with honey. In the dining room, the table is spread with a white damask cloth, then set with matching napkins and our best silverware, although it is not silver. At the table, no one yells, not even my father. If he starts in — that means picks a fight — my grandmother gives him the eye. "*Sha, Leon. Shabbos.*"

I love the hush of Friday nights, lighted candles and the flavors of my grandmother's kitchen spiraling through time.

Francis takes a bowl of poached white figs from the refrigerator. I hadn't known he'd prepared them earlier. A shudder of surprise and disappointment. He reads my thoughts, gives a shrug. "From yesterday."

A small betrayal. The feeling passes.

Pineapple rings, cut thick, simmer in butter and brown sugar. Francis shakes the pan. "It needs to caramelize a little bit." Again, Jo appears. He glances her way and, before she asks, declares, "*Ah, très bon*." Then, to me *sotto voce*, he confides, "She loves figs."

Jo nods.

Careful not to look at Francis, I turn to Jo. "I do, too."

*****

Francis has selected blue and white porcelain dessert bowls, each with a chrysanthemum pattern. Squeezed between two narrow tables, I watch the back of his hand, his fine gray hairs, as he lifts each pineapple ring, drizzles sauce, then, with a flick of his wrist, rights the pan. Inside each bowl, the deep blue of chrysanthemums, the fruity yellow of pineapple, the caramel hue of sauce. Now, a pale poached fig in each center. What delicate balance of texture and color.

I speak, softly. "Do you like the beauty of food?"

Holding the pan, he pauses. "Ah yes, the aesthetic and the colors."

*****

Outside, I sit at the table. Francis pulls up a chair at the opposite end. Jo pours Armagnac, a brandy distilled nearby. She retreats inside. Perhaps she is uncomfortable with so much spoken English. Perhaps she's tired. She has sliced baguettes, opened wine bottles, cleared places and walked the length of the restaurant over and over. I see her in shadow, sitting alone at a table.

We talk and linger, until finally the sky turns the deep blue of the painted chrysanthemums inside our bowls. Tree branches hang in silhouette. Francis, speaking a mixture of English and French, tells a story of the years he spent in Arizona. "I took care of them all," he says, "Reid...

John, the photographer, interrupts. "Harry Reid?"

"Yes, yes," Francis says. "And Goldwater, the father. They're all the same."

So we talk of the follies of our politicians, their corruption and their greed, and because none of us wants to spoil this evening, we let our own foibles and losses float below the surface where no one sees. Jo returns, offering more Armagnac. We decline, stand to leave, kiss, kiss, the French way. "*Au revoir.*"

"*A bientôt.*" Soon.

The deep blue sky floats to darkness as we make our way along these cobbled streets, walking through the oldest passage, and I, so full, so well fed, understand that because we are visitors, we don't see Auvillar's underside, any more than we see each other's. Yet, something intangible lingers. Shadows of darkness dwell inside these cobbles and massive stones, the arch under the clock tower where once this village was gated, the Cathedral where in an adjacent graveyard the bones of the dead lie stacked, a vacant convent where early one morning in 1943, Gestapo looked for a Jewish child, all slumbering and still like giant cats curled beside warm stoves.

At Moulin à Nef, I pass the dark kitchen, then climb wooden stairs to my room, the taste of time and ginger on my tongue.

Sandell Morse's work has appeared in numerous publications, including, Creative Nonfiction, Ploughshares, the New England Review, Fourth Genre and Ascent. One of her essays, "Hiding," is listed in Best American Essays, 2013. "Houses" has been nominated for Best of the Net, 2014, and also for a Pushcart Prize. "Canning Jars" has won an honorable mention in the Soul-Making Keats Literary Competition, 2013. "Circling My Father" won the 2010 Michael Steinberg essay award. Morse has won awards for her work from Press 53 and the Maine Writers and Publishers Alliance. She has been a Tennessee Williams Scholar at the Sewanee Writers' Conference, an Associate Artist at the Atlantic Center for the Arts, and a Fellow at the Virginia Center for the Creative Arts. She is an avid skier, hiker and dog lover. She lives and writes on the coast of Maine.

LOST AT THE GRAND BAZAAR
Turkey

The moment I set foot in Istanbul, I wanted to lose myself in the maze of alleys and cul-de-sacs that zigzag inside the Grand Bazaar. Within hours of entering the vast marketplace, I truly was lost, swallowed whole by a labyrinth of hallways with rows of shops selling jewelry, turbans and silk clothing.

Directionless but no less curious, I wandered around, entranced. I ignored the shrill cries of beckoning merchants, drifted past storefronts draped with dried eggplant and okra hung like leis, and caught bits of chatter from the flowing crowd. I remember the strong tug on my arm from a man with deep-set ebony eyes. At first I thought he was offering directions, but soon it was clear that this chummy stranger was showing me to his carpet shop. I slipped back into the throng of shoppers, enveloped in its frenzied pace.

*****

It was mid-June, and I'd earned a two-week break from my first job out of college. My friend Liz and I decided to fly to Turkey. There we were, 48 hours later, piling off a steamy tour bus. The driver warned us to watch our wallets, travel in pairs, and "beware of the white slave trade." Those last words jarred me, but Liz shrugged them off.

"Don't believe him," she said. "He's just trying to spook us."

I smiled as we forded a rushing stream of bikes, buses, cars and taxicabs. This was to be a life-altering adventure in a world far removed from our own back in New York. The lure was more than just the ancient cobbled streets, the architectural wonders and the spicy aroma wafting from the kabob stands. I liked this city's otherworldly mystique. Istanbul, a historic crossroads where East meets West; the only world city globally straddling two continents. An asymmetrical mix of the past with the present. A perfect place for anything to happen.

I don't remember how we found the Kapali Carsi, the Grand Bazaar. Maybe it was the flurry of people and festive colors that pulled us in the right direction. Heady whiffs of cinnamon and cloves from a sweets shop dulled any warnings from the bus driver about self-guided tours. We were now in one of the largest and oldest covered markets in the world, with more than 4,000 shops at our fingertips.

"It's all too inviting," said Liz, "Why don't we explore a bit on our own before lunch?"

"Great! Let's meet at 1 o'clock in front of that quilt-making shop."

I nodded toward a pile of brightly-embroidered quilts closely guarded by a black-mustached salesman, gesturing me to come over. I pointed to my watch and said, "Sorry, no time." Two hours from now, I thought, maybe I'll be a match for these clever merchants. Liz waved as she disappeared down the twisting passageway.

As I turned to go the opposite way, I was caught in a wave of shoppers, tossed and jostled for yards before I surrendered to the tide. That's when I glimpsed a dress boutique at the far end of the corridor. Who could miss its protective evil eye hanging from a beam? I had seen these bright blue glass eyes everywhere: dangling from shop ceilings, car mirrors and pieces of jewelry. The minute I entered the boutique, I could feel the eye's penetrating stare. When I turned my back, the intensity of its power seemed to tap me on the shoulder. Hadn't I heard on the bus tour that the ancient Greeks and Romans believed the spell of the evil eye could cause injury, disease, and sometimes death?

But I was too drawn to the racks of crepe-like dresses to worry about calamity striking. I'd noticed that women wearing these flowing, sleeveless numbers seemed to take the mugginess of summer in stride. There I was traipsing along in a dark, silky Maggie of London dress, face glistening in the heat. And there were the Istanbul women, faces fresh and cool, as if they'd just left an air-conditioned spa.

Minutes later, the clerk was wrapping my selection in turquoise tissue paper, its vibrant yellow and red sun pattern peeking through the packaging. Now I could dress like I belonged here, I thought. I glanced at my watch: 11:45 a.m. I still had a while to stroll around. On the way out of the shop, I saluted the evil eye, hoping a little respect would pave a safe path.

Off to the left was a coffee stand where I ordered a cup of steaming espresso. I found a vacant spot on the floor parallel to the blur of shoppers streaming by, and sat cross-legged on the cool tiles, soothed by the swirling sound of a nearby fountain. Seconds later, a woman, who looked about 19 years old, sat down beside me. She was cradling a baby.

"Lady, please hold my baby while I get something to eat," she implored, touching my hand.

Before I could utter a word, the woman had placed her bundle in the crook of my arm and disappeared. The baby was wrapped in a cotton quilt with a pale pink-and-white pattern. She had wispy dark curls falling from her pink skull cap. Tiny silver studs in each earlobe gleamed like stars.

This was crazy. I had heard of such happenings in Acapulco while I was visiting. Child mothers unable to care for their young would ask unsuspecting strangers to watch them, and then leave the caregivers with an abandoned child. I prayed that this woman wasn't pulling such a stunt. OK, I thought, I'll give her 15 minutes. If she doesn't return by then, I'll take this baby to the police.

The minutes crept by. The baby slept peacefully, as I perused the crowd for her mother. I remembered she had tightly-braided, dark hair partially concealed by a paisley scarf.

"Oh, please come back," I pleaded silently. This was not how I wanted to embrace Istanbul. The baby stirred as I shifted her to my right shoulder. I glanced down at my watch, noting it was close to 12:30 p.m. Liz will never believe this, I thought.

From out of nowhere, the woman with mysterious ways did reappear. Smiling, she lifted her sleeping infant from my shoulder. What a rush of relief! My diplomatic duty for the day was done.

"Thank you, my friend," she said, shaking my hand. "I am so grateful." She pressed something smooth and silky against my palm. A bunch of red rose petals.

"Rose petals?" I asked. But the woman, again, had vanished. I wrapped the seven petals securely in a napkin and placed it in my purse.

My head was reeling from this strange encounter, but there was no time to rest. I had 30 minutes to find my way back to the quilt-making shop. Clutching my dress package, I pushed through a crush of shoppers. I moved like a daredevil running with the bulls, hurtling past merchants and dodging beggars and ragged hagglers. Darting from one point to the next, I looked for landmarks – anything familiar to confirm this was the right direction. Ah, I know this hallway with that leather wallet shop and the prominent SALE sign. I thought I also recognized some briefcases lining the route. But, within minutes, I reached a dead end. Now I understood what the guidebook meant by "chaotic order!"

What time was our cruise ship leaving port? I couldn't remember. It was already close to 1 o'clock, and I worried that Liz might not wait for me. An elderly woman and burly salesman bargained with intensity a few feet away. I rushed up to the pair, and asked directions.

"You are not far, Miss," said the salesman in fluent English. "Keep to the right for a few hundred meters, until you see a vendor selling flags. When you reach his shop, go left past the fez makers and, I believe, the next street on the right is the quilt-makers."

I listened carefully, hoping to find the way as straightforward as he described. Thanking him, I continued down the busy corridor past outlandish wares and dealers dueling in many tongues. The heat was suffocating as the walls narrowed. I needed to escape. Plowing through the masses, I knocked some shoppers off balance. What was I looking for? A fez vendor or was it flags?

Rounding a bend, I spotted a tall figure in the distance who seemed to be signaling me. The vendor with the flags! He looked as if he were waving me across the finish line. I kicked up my heels, bent on finding Liz and a way out of here.

No one could have missed the fez maker's shop. About 20 red felt caps with black tassels piled high in the window in the shape of a pyramid. A merchant out front modeled one of the funny-looking caps.

"Hey, we have hats for you, too, Miss. Have a look?"

I pretended not to hear him. I was focused on finding the quilt-makers' street, but dealers surrounded me at every step, trying to gain control. My ankles weighed me down, fully shackled and tied. I craved fresh air and open space.

Breaking free, I ran at full speed. My dress was damp with perspiration, clinging to me like a second skin. Let me out of this labyrinth, dear God; I've had enough! And – yes! - there it was: the third street on the right was the quilt-makers. It was now 1:30 p.m. If Liz was still around, it would be a bonus.

I sprinted by shopkeepers wanting to make contact. But I only had eyes for our designated meeting spot. All at once, I saw Liz's pale green dress down the street.

"Liz!"

She immediately turned, and ran my way. "Hey, where've you been?" she asked, giving me a hug. "I was about to file a missing person's report." Judging from her assortment of bags and her jubilant expression, I was certain she'd had a completely different experience from my own.

"Sorry," I said, collapsing on a bench. "I was incredibly lost. A trail of bread crumbs would've helped, but all I had were these rose petals," I laughed, pulling the small packet from my purse.

"Tell me all about it," said Liz, looking quizzically at the wrapped petals. "We still have another hour before our ship leaves."

"Let's find a taverna, drink wine and swap stories," I said between breaths.

As we approached a gate leading out of this mother-of-all marketplaces, Liz and I were stopped by two vendors who wrapped tiny skirts adorned with shiny gold spangles around our waists. We shook off the skirts, and headed for the exit. After two hours in this bazaar, their bold behavior didn't faze us.

Outside, it was cooler away from halls teeming with people and air heated by thousands of watts of electric bulbs. Following a narrow side street, we wandered about half a mile with the sun warming our backs, enjoying the mob-free peacefulness. Soon the lively strains of a bouzouki drifting from an open taverna window pulled us in, like old friends enticing us to visit.

Inside the rustic walls, a warm smile from a passing waiter was as welcoming as the music. Liz and I seated ourselves at a corner table by a window overlooking a garden of red and yellow tulips. Signaling the waiter, we ordered two glasses of Sarafin chardonnay. Then, I plucked the tightly folded napkin out of my purse, eager to decipher the meaning of its contents.

I shook the napkin open and let the red petals fall, soft and delicate, onto the white tablecloth. Their fragrance was as fresh and honeysuckle-sweet as the quilt of the swaddled infant.

"Any idea what these mean?" I asked Liz, relaying my experience with the young mother who'd slipped them in my hand after watching her baby. Liz looked at me in disbelief and laughed.

"To new ports and beginnings!" I said, raising my glass. The bouzouki player cheered, as our wine glasses clinked.

The staccato rhythm continued, prompting patrons to the dance floor. Hands high above my head, I snapped my fingers and twirled about as free-floating as the rose petals onto the tablecloth. I had found my way home again.

Dorothy Maillet is a freelance writer living in Irvington, NY. She has a penchant for exploring the world and its people. Her stories have appeared in www.more.com, www.bootsnall.com and Westchester Life, as well as in various publications of the Gannett newspaper chain.

MY OWN TWO FEET
USA

We've all been to that place. When things get really tough, the most tantalizing option is to flee. But I couldn't. Not yet. But soon.

Over the past several months, I had fallen into a deep depression. I worked alone at home as my business partner and I had parted ways. My outdoorsy and emotionally bankrupt boyfriend had not worked out. Conversely, I was on my second and third round of maid of honor duty for two friends. And I was living in my mother's basement.

To survive, I binged on Ben & Jerry's and Netflix.

I had reached a crossroads. I felt like an outsider in Chicago. At 29 I was lost, confused and miserable.

I didn't know why, but I needed to go.

Ironically, the idea of where to go came from an unexpected place. My emotionally bankrupt ex. Funny how that works. That jerk, who was always talking about how he had hiked the Appalachian Trail, gave me the best idea of my life.

Hiking a 2,180-mile trail that spanned 14 states seemed like the perfect way to escape and find myself at the same time. That's it, I decided. I was going to do it.

My family didn't take the news well. In particular, my mother. In my naivety, I thought she would get over it. Desperate to save money since I was electing to go without a job or home for several months, I moved into her basement. Big mistake.

Every day, she barraged me with acidic criticism.

"This is a stupid idea. You're making a huge mistake."

She was panicked for my safety and determined to deter me from my goal. She thought if she badgered me enough, I would change my mind. It didn't work.

Let me explain my qualifications for taking on such a task. I was a city girl with no outdoors or hiking experience to speak of, without so much as a tent or backpack to my name. In fact, I was a Girl Scout dropout and had only camped a handful of times in my life — all within range of a working toilet. I couldn't navigate even while using GPS, and the thought of sleeping alone in the forest at night terrified me.

But I knew I could do this. Sticking to my guns, I started preparing.

I found books and documentaries on the Appalachian Trail, and joined a trail hikers forum where other aspiring thru-hikers (anyone who completes the entire trail in less than one year) compared notes and planning information. I read about Grandma Gatewood, the legendary hiker who in 1955, alone and at 67, thru-hiked the trail in Keds with a bag slung over her shoulder. If she could hike the Appalachian Trail in retirement why couldn't I?

A couple thousand dollars later I had a tent, sleeping pad, down sleeping bag, backpack, water purification drops, trekking sticks, camping stove, mosquito head net, DEET bug spray, freeze-dried meals, a flask of Jameson, and an assortment of other outdoor supplies. I found pants that zipped off at the knee and merino wool socks, a world away from my high-heeled city life.

The Appalachian Trail has a northern terminus on Mount Katahdin in Maine, then stretches south through 13 additional states until completing its course on the summit of Springer Mountain in Georgia. Each year, 2,000 optimistic hikers attempt to complete the trail. One in four actually do.

Obligations kept me from starting the trail in Georgia, where the terrain is easier, allowing hikers to comfortably grow their "trail legs." The other option is to start in the most challenging state, Maine, and head south.

Heading south from the summit of Mount Katahdin, after several miles the trail enters the legendary and unforgiving 100-mile wilderness. Once you enter this remote stretch, it's nearly impossible to get out any way other than on foot.

I was excited but scared out of my mind. I confided my trepidation to my friend Jess, and she decided to hike the first section with me. I could have kissed her feet and kicked my heels in the air.

The day we flew to Maine, my mom dropped me off at the airport. Through choked tears, she hugged me.

"You're so stubborn."

I didn't know what to say. It was so much easier to be mad at her when she was mean. Now that I saw the pain and heartache behind it all, I felt horribly guilty. But I knew as soon as I turned toward the airport, I was free. After a long hug, I kissed her goodbye.

After a bus ride, we arrived at our final destination of the day, a local hiker lodge filled with other Appalachian Trail hikers. I didn't know it then, but some of the friends I made that first day would be the same people I was with on my last.

Three hikers stood out in particular. We met Brooks at the bus stop and assumed he was a hiker based on the telltale backpack, scruffy beard and hiking boots. He was from Tennessee, and had left a lucrative and successful corporate career behind. Before the trail he had completed a survival course that would make British adventurer Bear Grylls look like a girly girl, and worked at an outfitter to get his gear at a discount. He had also completed EMT and wilderness first responder courses. I decided that in the interest of my personal safety, I would make him my new best friend.

A couple from Colorado, Holly and Brian, had come to hike the trail together. She had left behind an exhausting job as a high school teacher, and he had left a coveted tech job in the banking industry. They had done every outdoor activity you could think of — hiking, skiing, mountain biking, trail running, snowshoeing, kayaking — it blew my mind. Brian had grown up in the Midwest like me, so we hit it off immediately.

All three of them were like me — they had come to the trail to complete a goal and had no idea what came next. But they knew the life they lived before was not something they wanted to repeat.

The next day, a group of us began our hike to the summit of Mount Katahdin. To reach the 5,269-foot summit, a 10-mile round-trip hike is required. For each of the five miles leading up to the summit, elevation climbs 1,000 feet per mile.

As I started hiking, a feeling of exhilaration and disbelief flooded my body. After months of planning, I was taking my first of what would become hundreds of thousands of steps.

My foray into the unknown had begun.

Breathing in the crisp Maine air, I was astounded at the beauty around me. I could hear birds chirping in the tops of towering trees. Summer sunlight filtered through the branches to the ground. I felt so happy to be walking on the dirt and through those trees. For once, I wasn't getting a city-sized slice of nature — I was completely encompassed by the wilderness. Moose, beaver, and bear replaced the city rats of my recent past.

The hike to the summit was tiring and, as the miles passed, I got a taste of what it would feel like to hike all day. My quads burned, my heart raced, and before long, my feet ached. The trail, led by white blaze markers, guided the path and tree roots and rocks littered the trail. Trying my best to avoid the obstacles, I still found myself tripping often. On the mountain summit, 50 mph winds whipped my face as I held tight to the Mount Katahdin sign. I had officially begun my Appalachian Trail thru-hike.

With a feeling of purpose, I began the slow descent. My knees throbbed from the impact of each step, but the physical pain and exhaustion felt good. All of the anguish and depression that had built for months was finally able to begin its release.

That night at camp, I dived into my freeze-dried meal with mouthwatering fervor. Spaghetti and meatballs in a bag never tasted so good. When I took off my shoes, I saw several blisters. It was a relief to give my feet some fresh air. After setting up my tent for the first night on the trail, I fell into a deep sleep on my inflatable sleeping pad.

The next day, accompanied by my backbreaking 55-pound backpack, I set out toward the beginning of the 100-mile wilderness. I had been terrified of running out of food and supplies, and now my overstuffed backpack was bursting at the seams.

As my shoulder blades strained against the load, I wondered how I would carry the weight.

Trekking on, I felt at peace in my surroundings. The magnitude of the wilderness was unlike anything I had ever experienced. And with each crunch of leaves under my shoes, I was reminded of my progress.

But at the end of the day, each step felt like an eternity. I had never been so exhausted. Then a sign would alert me of the shelter ahead, and I found the energy to finish the day.

I had read about the shelters on the trail, but I wasn't prepared for the reality. Imagine a wooden box with one side removed. They can usually fit 10-15 people if they are lined up like sardines in their sleeping bags. There are 250 shelters along the trail roughly 10-15 miles apart. Each had its own characteristics: Some looked like log cabins, others had elaborate stone fireplaces, but most were simple wooden structures. But for a tired hiker at the end of the day, each shelter was like a Four Seasons hotel.

If you reached a shelter in time to snag a spot for your sleeping bag, you probably also had a place to hang your food without needing to throw a bear line (provided no bear activity had been reported, otherwise hanging your food above your head is a bad idea). You also didn't have to set up your tent, which meant that you could go to sleep faster and not deal with packing up a damp tent in the morning. The cons were that you didn't have any personal space. You might wake up and find yourself inches from another hiker's face. And if you can't sleep with eight people snoring around you, set up your tent.

To take care of your number one and two business, you had two options. The first was to dig a hole off the trail, out of sight, and do what you had to do. The other was to use the privies at the shelters. As a single gal surrounded by mostly guys, I usually opted for the privy. Going to the bathroom in a privy requires strategy and strength. Some of the doors swing shut and if you don't like going to the bathroom in the dark, you need to hold the door open while also hovering over the hole, holding your breath, clutching your toilet paper and waving away flies. If you hear someone coming, you get to add shouting "Occupied!" to your list.

Each shelter has a trail journal, which is the hiker's edition of US Weekly. The journals reported who got on the trail, who got off and why, who is hiking with whom, and gossip about the jerk who keeps tagging the shelters (so not cool, Peter Pan Pyro). Everyone in the trail journal signs with their trail name (Hulk, Can't Stop, Skittles, Blueberry Piss Licker, Black Eagle, Furnace, Just Jill, Little Big Wind, Lone Star, Fauna, to name a few) and then their trail direction and year (I was SOBO —short for southbound — 2010). Receiving a trail name can happen to you on day one or one month in. From that point forward, you are known only as your trail name.

The days were filled with chattering among new friends or hiking alone with your thoughts. Everyone was a new friend with a new story.

Although we talked about careers, school, where we grew up and our experiences in the outdoors, we mostly talked about two topics — food and food.

Hiking for eight hours a day turns your body into a calorie-burning furnace. I was always hungry. Adding extra calories to each meal was the only way to slow down the constant need to strap on a feedbag. Ramen noodles with spray butter. Peanut butter spread between two raspberry Pop-Tarts. Summer sausage tossed into powdered mashed potatoes. Chocolate bars that need to be licked out of their wrapper in the summer heat. We used food in a barter system — with the surrender of a tuna packet, you could become the proud owner of an Oreo four-pack. Unfortunately, no one wanted my tuna packets.

Everyone came to the trail with different gear. All day we argued in favor of whatever gear choice we had made, kind of like a hiker pissing contest. Within the great gear debate, most topics centered around base weight and product quality.

Other hikers bragged about how low their backpack weight was, while I began quietly evaluating what I could get rid of. Then there was the water purification argument analyzing the most effective and lightweight tools for cleaning water, followed by the typical sharing of any unfortunate Giardia experiences from those who hadn't treated their water properly.

Some thought a tent was a waste of weight and space, and that a simple tarp would suffice. No protection from spiders and mosquitoes at night? No thanks. Other hikers thought frame backpacks were outdated and cumbersome. Each minute detail was exhaustively debated, ranging from the many uses of duct tape and how much water to carry. Separate factions believed trail running shoes were best, while others argued hiking boots were better.

In this last debate, I had been a strong supporter of the trail running shoe team, but I was now having doubts. Wanting to wear something lightweight that would allow me to be agile, a trail running shoe had seemed like the best idea. I had settled on a black and green shoe that came with a malleable sole and breathable mesh upper.

But as the past four days had unfolded, my blisters had gotten worse. Several had sprouted on six of my toes, and one stubborn blister near my heel swelled with each step.

I had also noticed something that I had long suspected. I was clumsy.

Cautious with each step, I clung insecurely to my trekking poles. The roots and rocks were a labyrinth of danger, and I was terrified I would fall down a boulder and break my leg. I didn't want my journey to end before it began.

My ankles rolled all day long. The amount of tripping and stumbling was alarming. My trail running shoes offered no toe protection when I tripped on rocks, and as my feet wrenched around their flimsy shells, I knew I had chosen poorly.

One night, after breaking down into tears over my growing blisters, I overheard six words from a New York hiker (who was constantly begging for food handouts) that ignited further anger and determination.

"She's not going to make it."

Through my tears, I thought: screw that guy. He didn't know me. And he didn't even know how to pack his own food. (I later found out that he was not an Appalachian Trail hiker, but a homeless guy posing as a hiker. Which explained the begging. Live and learn.)

But even with that guy in the picture, the best part of the trail isn't the nature, it's the people. Hikers quickly become your family. Out there in the woods, all you have is each other. You take care of each other. You help someone set up their tent, they help you collect water. You hang your food bags together and share a pep talk along the way. Their friendship holds you accountable to your goal. Each day I was able to keep going because of their support.

My nightly popping of blisters provided some relief, but as I assessed the raw meat that my feet had become, I felt helpless. In my trail preparation efforts, I had loaded up on Band-Aids, gauze, sanitizer, moleskin, antibiotic ointment and duct tape.

When the Band-Aids and ointment didn't stop the blisters from getting bigger, I switched to moleskin. They swelled larger. I added gauze, thinking the extra padding would protect. They grew. Desperate, I stuck duct tape on them after another hiker promised me it was foolproof. It wasn't. The next day, they had reached gargantuan proportions.

One was causing more trouble than the rest. Near my inner right heel, one blister continued to swell. All day when I hiked, I cursed that damn blister. It was incredibly painful. I thought if I could just drain it, I would feel better. But my safety pin didn't make a difference no matter how many times I stabbed.

When I asked if anyone had any advice, they had a different idea in mind. They thought my trail name should be Tumor Toe.

"No. Damn. Way."

They agreed to give me another name. As the miles passed and we talked about the possibilities, it was decided I should be Day Tripper. Since I couldn't seem to walk straight, the name was fitting. It was perfect.

And from that moment forward, I was Day Tripper.

A hiker named Mountain Goat for his agility, despite a crippling 75-pound backpack, offered to come to my aid. He had come to the trail with razor blades, gloves and iodine. He promised to clean the wound and be gentle.

Scared but desperate, I agreed. I had three more days until I was out of the 100-mile wilderness, and I didn't know if I could make it with my feet the way they were. Closing my eyes, I let him slice.

I felt relief as the blister drained, and afterward I was a new woman. I tackled the day and settled into camp without my blister-popping ritual that night.

But when I woke up, I had a new problem.

Another pain had started. As I looked closer, I saw dirt under my skin. I had put on clean socks and kept my foot bandaged, but hours of hiking made it impossible to keep the wound sterile.

As the day went on, the pain became worse. My hiking slowed and I started walking on the outside of my foot.

The next day, it was rainy and cold. The rain made me more nervous about falling on rock, making my footing even more unsteady. When I got into camp that night, the wound was beginning to look red and was sensitive to touch.

An infection. In my inexperience, I hadn't even considered this as a possibility.

Before I could get antibiotics, I had to hike 15 miles to the road and hitchhike to town.

In the meantime, the pressure on my blister felt like an elephant balancing on the head of a needle. Each step was excruciating. I began chowing down Ibuprofen like candy.

By midday, my hiking friends were ready for town.

"We love you! See you soon!"

And just like that, I was on my own.

I wavered between staying positive and feeling defeated.

I dreamed of the delicious food and hot shower waiting for me. Clean socks and a fresh shirt. I imagined my new friends next to me as I hiked, cheering me on.

'C'mon Gina, keep going!"

"You got this. Only a little farther!"

"I know you can do it. Don't stop moving!"

But the pain was getting worse, and no amount of Ibuprofen was helping. The pain soured my positive thoughts. Out of all the hikers, I was the slowest. In the first week, I had destroyed my shoes and feet, and picked up an infection. My inexperience was stark. Jess had taken to the trail like a fish to water.

If this was a contest of the survival of the fittest, I would be the dinner to the lions.

I felt security and happiness with my new friends, but this injury would leave me in town as they moved on. Jess would go home. I would be alone.

What if everyone is right? What if I had made a horrible mistake thinking I could do this?

The sun was setting, and I still had three miles to hike before the road. I didn't want to be alone in the forest while everyone else was in town. But the pain and fatigue made my legs feel like lead.

Step by step, I told myself to keep going. Just keep going. Believe that you will make it out by dark. Don't slow down. Keep going and ignore the pain. You can't get out tonight unless you believe you will. Keep hiking.

Racing against dusk, I felt a burst of hope as I heard cars. The path opened and a road came into view.

Hobbling toward the road, I collapsed on a boulder and sobbed. My mind and body were overwhelmed.

Tears streaming down my face, I shoved a thumb into the road. A car pulled over immediately. Struggling to compose myself and failing miserably, I stepped into the backseat of an elderly couple with teardrops falling off my chin. Between my sobs I thanked them while they offered encouraging words and told me about their granddaughter.

"Our granddaughter is into this outdoors stuff. She did a triathlon and was a top finisher!"

Wiping my eyes, I thanked them again as I hauled my pack over my shoulders. I had arrived. I got my first glimpse of what life would be like in Monson, ME, population 1,000. It was the quintessential small American town.

My friends were waiting at the Lakeshore House, which offered a Laundromat, rooms for rent and a bar and restaurant all in one place. Walking in, I was overcome with joy when I saw all of my friends.

"You made it! Give me a hug!"

"We have a pizza coming for you, here's a beer!"

"Want the rest of my sundae?"

I was so relieved and happy I thought my face would break from smiling.

A few minutes later, sipping beer with my feet dangling from the bar stool, a song came on the radio. I stopped mid-sip. My arms and legs prickled as the lyrics filled the air.

> *Got a good reason for taking the easy way out*
> *Got a good reason for taking the easy way out now*

I stared at the speaker in the corner of the bar. I wanted to make sure my ears weren't playing tricks on me. To make sure the blisters hadn't induced an auditory hallucination. But no. The music played on.

> *She was a day tripper, a one way ticket yeah*
> *It took me so long to find out, and I found out*

It was my song. My trail name. It was "Day Tripper."

The Beatles recorded 275 songs in the span of their history. 275 songs. And mine just happened to play on the local radio station in small-town Maine, precisely as I sat down to enjoy the best slice of pizza a Laundromat/restaurant had ever served.

Who knew a song about dropping acid could feel so much like the hand of God? But there it was.

At that moment, I knew.

I had made the right choice. Everything was going to be okay. I was going to keep hiking. I would make it.

Travel writer Gina Kremer of Denver has an insatiable thirst for adventure. During her travels she has acci-

dentally stepped into the northern side of the military demarcation line in South Korea, strapped on crampons to hike glaciers in Iceland, and roamed Burning Man on a cruiser bike. To view her work visit www.ginakremer.com.

NEVER TOO OLD TO JUMP
New Zealand

"Five" — What was I thinking?

"Four" — At my age, I could easily change my mind — just tell them I don't want to do this.

"Three" — They could take off the harness and I could just walk away.

"Two" — I could get my money back.

"One" — I jumped.

It all started on Vanuatu, or so the story goes. Hundreds of years ago, on one of the 83 islands in that South Pacific archipelago nation, a young wife was pursued to the top of a towering banyan tree by her jealous husband. To escape him, she jumped to the ground far below. Her husband jumped after her to his death. The woman, however, lived, saved by the jungle vines from the tree that she had managed to tie to her ankles.

Over the centuries, this story has inspired countless men to practice jumping from tall places, just in case they should ever be in a situation like that of the hapless husband. Today some jump to celebrate the harvest and prove their manhood.

So what was I proving on this fine spring day in Queenstown, New Zealand? Ten years earlier a young mother I knew had bungy-jumped in a maternal effort to show her children that you could conquer your fears, that even though she was terrified of jumping into the ether held only by an oversized rubber band, she would do it. At the time I thought how brave and admirable she was to have done this for her children — and how happy I was that this was not something I ever intended — or needed — to do. Now, at 73, I had reached the point where I didn't have to prove anything to anyone, and jumping into space sounded like something no sane person would do.

However, after two full days in this beautiful lake-front, mountain-rimmed town, my husband Mark and I had done all that we wanted to do here. We were ready to move on, but our flight schedule was set; we had one more day here.

As I was drifting off to sleep that second night, a vision jumped into my mind of the young man I had seen that afternoon bungy jumping off a platform near the top of the gondola lift to the top of Bob's Peak. I woke up with bungy on my mind. "Why do you want to do this?" Mark asked with a bemused smile on our morning walk up the winding trail of Queenstown Hill. The more we talked, the more appealing the idea became. I had set myself other goals late in life — like trekking in the Himalayas in my 50s and running my first (and probably only) marathon to celebrate my 60th birthday. I loved the idea that although any reporter would describe me as "elderly," I could still undertake new (and, at least in this case, nutty) challenges.

We walked into the office of AJ Hackett Bungy Tours. AJ took his first bungy jump from Auckland's Greenhithe Bridge in 1986, went on to jump from other bridges and other high places, including the Eiffel Tower. He is the major commercial operator worldwide, and advertises that he has never had a fatality among his jumpers. The word bungy, he has said, is Kiwi (New Zealander) slang for elastic.

As I was asking Aimmee, the young receptionist, questions such as how jumpers are connected to the bungy cord (answer: by the ankles or in a harness); whether I would have to dive head first (no: in the harness I could jump upright); what were the differences among the four jump sites in the Queenstown area (mostly variations in height of jump and distance from town), and how much the adventure cost ($103 U.S. plus $50 for photos and DVD of my jump), I was still only gathering information, not making a commitment.

Aimmee smiled and then said hesitantly, "I'm going to ask you a rude question." I correctly anticipated her query: "How old are you?" Would I have to sign a spe-

cial release? Take out extra insurance? Tell them where
to send the body should I ruin Hackett's record? "Oh,
good," she smiled at my answer. "Since you're over 65
we have a special discount!"

Not a rude question, after all. I could ride the gondola
up to the platform, jump, and get a T-shirt, photos and a
DVD of my adventure, all for $64, less than half-price.
The prospect of such a bargain outweighed the butterflies in my stomach.

A couple of hours later Mark and I rode the gondola
up and crossed a narrow foot bridge to AJ Hackett's little office in the air. Here I stepped on a scale (minimum
weight for jumpers is 35 kilos (77 pounds); maximum,
130 kgs (286 pounds). Aside from the public embarrassment of having my weight written on the back of my
hand for all to see, there was no problem. I gave my
medical history, including rotator cuff surgery eight
months before. No problem here either.

To quote AJ: "Physically, no harm will come to a
jumper. The system is very gentle on a person who
jumps." Hmmm. If no harm could come to a jumper,
why did I have to sign papers agreeing to hold AJ Hackett Bungy harmless from any personal injury, damage or
trauma to myself?

At the platform a cheerful young man asked me
where I was from (was he trying to distract me from full
awareness of what I was doing?) as he helped me into
my climber-type harness, which was like stepping into a
pair of shorts consisting of belts and buckles. He at-

tached me by a ring on my harness to the rubber bungy cord, tailor-made to the jumper's body weight.

My "handler" told me to walk to the edge of the platform and smile for the camera. I did as I was told; I had temporarily suspended thinking for myself. Then he told me to step back on the platform, he would count down from five — and I would run to the edge and then leave what was now passing for terra firma to plunge into the firmament.

"Five. Four. Three. Two. One."

My stomach lurched as I fell into the air 140 feet. The glories of Lake Wakatipu were below me but I couldn't look at anything. I knew that Mark was taking my photo but I couldn't smile for the camera. My only thoughts revolved around the dizzying sensation of dropping.

And then, after my two seconds of free fall, I felt myself being held firmly, comfortingly by the bungy cord. My stomach stopped somersaulting as I bounced up, and then down, in a gentle swinging motion. Euphoria replaced terror. I looked over to where Mark stood. I smiled. I waved. I swung around. I kept bouncing.

I looked down and around. I saw the snow-capped peaks of the Remarkables mountain range, the glacial blue lake, the serpentine curve of the forested shoreline, and the buildings of Queenstown. I bounced and swung some more. I marveled at the absolute silence, the feeling of being alone in the air, and the sensation of flying. And then, all too soon — was my adventure over already? — I saw the other cord come down, the one I had to catch and link to my harness so I could be winched back up to the platform. This one was swinging away from me, and I briefly wondered how I would get out of outer space if I didn't manage to clasp it. I connected it, I was hoisted up, and my much-too-short ride of only 3 ½ minutes was over.

My thrill at having done this was, it struck me later, out of all proportion to the feat itself. It had not required months of training (like the trekking and the marathon). It had not required any special skill or effort. It demanded nothing more of me than the ability to trust in technology and be willing to take a measured risk. But, as Helen Keller once wrote, "Security is mostly a superstition. Avoiding danger is no safer in the long run than outright exposure. Life is either a daring adventure or nothing."

I did feel as if I had experienced a daring adventure, and as I hugged my husband I felt exhilarated and triumphant as I ticked off one more fear that I had conquered, and began to think about others that I had never even dreamed of facing.

As a grandmother, I like to think of myself as a mature, wise, elder. As a woman, I like the idea that I can still do something off the wall — or, in this case, off the platform. The words of a grizzled gypsy I had met 20 years earlier at a gathering of the hippie group the Rainbow Family of Living Light came to mind: "Everybody has to grow old, but you can stay immature forever."

Sally Wendkos Olds (sallywendkosolds.com) has written extensively about intimate relationships, personal growth and developmental issues throughout the life cycle, and has won national awards for both her book and magazine writing. In addition to her classic, The Complete Book of Breastfeeding, first published in 1972 and revised for its fourth edition in 2010, she is the author of 10 other books, including Super Granny: Great Stuff to Do with Your Grandkids and A Balcony in Nepal: Glimpses of a Himalayan Village. She is currently writing a book for people whose life partner has died a year or more previously.

HERE WE ARE
France

For her 13th birthday, I bought my daughter Lilia her very own suitcase, decorated with hot air balloon and artist palette motifs, in anticipation of a trip to Paris that we would take from our home in Japan a few months later. Now, as we counted the days to our departure, I thought about what we should pack.

Paris is a fashionable city. According to one blogger, the better dressed you are, the better the service. I, for one, was looking forward to dressing up. For my daughter, this trip would be a chance to eschew the navy polyester blazer, plaid pants and white shirt with ribbon that she wore every day as her uniform at the School of the Deaf. She would be free to assemble the funky outfits that she liked and show them off on the Champs-Elysses.

I'd managed to get us a reservation for dinner on Wednesday evening at Le Jules Verne on the second level of the Eiffel Tower. This had given me the perfect excuse to buy the gold sequined dress I'd been eyeing in a catalog. Lilia needed something special, too, so we went shopping at the nearby mall and found a lovely deep pink dress with tiered ruffles down the front. Shoes, however, were a problem.

Shoes had always been a problem. When clothing catalogs arrived in the mail, Lilia, at 6, would get out a red pen and circle the things she liked. Sometimes she circled pink pants or T-shirts with winsome prints, but usually it was the footwear: black patent dress shoes with bows, red suede Mary Janes, sandals with cut-out hearts.

The thing is, my daughter didn't need these kinds of shoes, nor could she wear them. Because of her cerebral palsy, she flexed her foot when she should be relaxing it. She tended to curl her toes, so to get any kind of shoes on her feet I had to slide my fingers underneath her soles and ease them in, making the cowgirl boots she coveted pretty much impossible. Once on, her shoes were always falling off. There was always someone running after us in shopping malls, down the sidewalk, in grocery stores, holding up one of the sneakers that had slipped off Lilia's foot.

Lilia was most secure in her $1,000-plus custom-made leg braces, which went all the way up to her knees. While wearing them, she could manage to go up and down stairs, and since, according to the Eiffel Tower website, she'd have to climb a stair or two to get onto the elevator, these would be most practical for dinner at Alain Ducasse's Michelin-starred, formal dress-required restaurant. However, the braces didn't go with her purple dress. They were clunky and bright orange. I always let her pick the color. (Her last pair, the year before, had been purple.) The orange was indeed pretty and bright, but the color clashed with most of her clothes.

I've noticed that Lilia usually doesn't want to wear them in public on weekends. I think maybe she's self-conscious.

So, at the mall she tried on a pair of black patent leather Mary Janes, but couldn't get them to stay on her feet. At the appropriately named Monet shoe store, Lilia found a pair of dark shoes decorated with leather blossoms. They were kind of expensive, but there was a strap that went around the ankle, and a zipper in back.

The staff hovered behind us as I helped Lilia ease off her nylon boots and worked her feet into the shoes. I knew they were ready to jump in and help, but Lilia's feet aren't like other people's. Finally, she was ready to stand. The shoes were a little big, and I wasn't sure that her toes would stay tucked in, but she insisted that they were comfortable. She said that they fit. I helped her to stand, and she nodded eagerly. I took a look at the price tag and frowned. Still, they were cheaper than custom-made braces, and they would go well with the dress.

"We'll take these," I told the clerk, who packed them in a shoe box printed with an image of Claude Monet's "The Bridge at Argenteuil."

I bought a pair of leopard print pumps with 4-inch heels to go with my dress, and we headed home. My husband and son had gone out of town for a baseball game, so for dinner we had sandwiches made with French cheese, and *tarte tatin* for dessert. We were practicing for Paris.

At Lilia's request, I'd booked us a hotel within view of the Eiffel Tower. By day we took in the Louvre, the Palace of Versailles and the Seine River by barge. In the evening, we ate dinner made from ingredients purchased at the Monoprix supermarket next door and watched the lights sparkling on the tower every hour after dark.

By Wednesday morning, Lilia had had enough of sightseeing. She just wanted to hang out in our hotel room, connect with her social network in Japan, and draw.

"But this is our last free day!" I told her. The next afternoon we would be joining children's book writers and illustrators for a three-day conference. This was our last chance to visit the Orsay Museum, one of the places I'd always wanted to see but had never quite gotten around to on my previous trips to Paris. Although I realized I was behaving like a Japanese tour guide, trying to cram as many sights and experiences into as little time as possible, I'd really been looking forward to the Orsay.

"We'll just go to one museum," I promised. "Tomorrow we'll stay in our room until noon. And the day after, you can play games and read manga (Japanese comics) on the tablet all you like."

I'd be busy attending workshops and schmoozing with fellow writers, so that would work out just fine. But not today.

I'd checked out the location, and it looked about a 30-minute walk from our hotel. The sun was shining, perfect for a stroll while I pushed Lilia in her wheelchair.

Hordes of visitors were outside the Orsay — tour groups from abroad, along with students on school excursions. We found the accessible entrance, then followed arrows to elevators, and went down secret passages. No one was around to direct us. When we finally got inside the crowded galleries, Lilia became grumpy because she wasn't allowed to take photos. I pointed out the Degas ballerinas, the painting that appeared on the Monet shoe box, and another painting by Claude Monet of the Rouen Cathedral, which we'd seen the day before.

She was only mildly interested. She perked up, however, when we came across a woman at an easel, painting her version of a Renoir landscape. We stood for a few minutes watching her mix paint on her palette and dab colors on the canvas. And then it was time for lunch.

Like the Louvre, the Orsay Museum consisted of many levels and many elevators, each going to a specific location. It took a while to figure out how to get to the restaurant, but when we finally did we were immediately whisked to a table. Next to us was a lone young Japanese woman, digging into a plate of steak and potatoes, several cameras and phones arrayed on the table before her.

The dining room was beautiful — all gilt and chandeliers. A peacock was painted above us, and huge arched windows admitted golden light. Bottles of wine were chilling on ice at the center of the room. The staff wore white shirts and black aprons.

We put in our order for peach nectar and the plat du jour. While we were waiting for our food to arrive, I asked Lilia, "Why have you been so grumpy?"

"It's embarrassing," she signed. "All those naked bodies."

Ah, the nudes. I hadn't realized she found them so disturbing. Stupid me. There were nude sculptures all over the town where we lived — in front of the public library, at the corner of the town hall's parking lot, inside lobbies. They were by a renowned local sculptor. She'd never seemed embarrassed by these bathing women, but she was now at the age when girls become self-conscious.

"OK, no more naked bodies." I promised her a polar bear after lunch. "Ours Blanc" by Francois Pompon was somewhere in this building.

Lunch was fish in cream sauce, accompanied by noodles flavored with lemongrass. With our big dinner at the Eiffel Tower that evening, we should have had just a little snack. But it was too late. The food was there be-

fore us, then in our stomachs. We had *iles flottantes* —
"floating islands" — for dessert.

Lilia was in a better mood after lunch. I was careful
to steer her away from the nudes as we ventured in
search of the polar bear, or the Van Goghs.

We never did make it to the big white bear, but after
asking directions a few times we managed to locate the
correct elevator for the Van Gogh exhibit. We got off on
a deserted corridor and passed through a door that
opened into the gallery. There on the wall was the por-
trait of Vincent Van Gogh in blue — the real one, as
opposed to the replica we'd seen before in a museum
near our house in Japan. Having accomplished part of
our quest, I suggested that we go back to our hotel to rest
up for the evening ahead.

Back at our hotel room, I took a shower and helped
Lilia into her tights. She put on her dress and the new
shoes with the leather blossoms on the ankle straps. I
shimmied into my gold sequined dress and leopard-print
heels. We took photos of each other.

The Eiffel Tower was only 15 or 20 minutes from our
hotel on foot, but I knew we might need a little extra
time to flag down a taxi. Plus, I hadn't really practiced
walking in those 4-inch heels, except for one trip from
my front door to the mailbox back in Japan. I needed to
step cautiously. We set out for the taxi stand with half an
hour to spare. We hadn't even crossed the street before
Lilia's left shoe fell off. Dressing up had made her more

nervous than usual, I figured. Her feet kept tensing up. The other shoe was hanging on by the ankle strap.

Lucky us — there was a guy sitting in his cab, eating fast food. After crumpling the wrapper and brushing his hands, he got out to help us.

"Her shoe…" he said.

"I know." I picked it up from the ground and helped Lilia into the taxi. Already, she had a run in her tights.

The driver heaved the collapsed wheelchair into the trunk.

"*A la Tour Eiffel!*" I said, working Lilia's foot back into the shoe.

She pouted, and I could tell that she was already regretting our choice of footwear.

The driver let us off near the carousel. For some reason, I expected someone to be waiting there, ready to help us. I'd specifically mentioned the wheelchair when making my reservation. And since this dinner was going to cost more than our family's monthly food budget, I didn't think a little assistance was too much to ask.

Hunched over because of the extra height, I pushed the wheelchair around to the entrance and found a few of our fellow diners. They were assembled at the steps leading to Le Jules Verne. To my dismay, some of them were dressed casually. I had already decided that the shoes — both mine and Lilia's — were a bad idea. Why hadn't I let her wear her braces? Who cares if scuffed orange clashed with purple?

Finally, a restaurant worker appeared. We would be taking a private elevator to the second level of the tower. To get to the elevator, we had to go up those stairs. I put Lilia's foot back into her shoe, and struggling a bit in my 4-inch heels, held her hand as she stepped up the stairs. Then a man in black pants and a white shirt helped me carry the wheelchair to the first landing.

"Her shoe…" the man said.

"Yes, I know." I picked it up. As I crouched beside Lilia, putting the shoe back onto her foot, I hoped that I wasn't flashing anyone. The gold sequined dress stopped at my thighs; it wasn't made for squatting. Sweat beaded at my hairline.

Inside, there was a small dark vestibule, with a steampunk feel — all grinding gears and period posters, apropos for a restaurant devoted to France's most famous science fiction writer.

Lilia's shoes fell off again. I gave up and carried the pair in my hand.

We went up in the elevator in small groups, along with the taciturn operator. There were more stairs leading to the elevator, but this time two men carried Lilia, wheelchair and all, up to the top.

I felt a flash of guilt. We shouldn't have come. This place was clearly inaccessible, and now we were importuning these men in white shirts and black bow ties. We were being burdensome. And once inside, what if Lilia accidentally spilled something, as she sometimes did at home? What if she broke a dish? Or exclaimed loudly?

But then I quickly shoved these thoughts aside. Lilia had just as much of a right to enjoy a meal in a nice restaurant as the next person. Just as much right as that teen tourist in casual clothes, who also was waiting with her family to board the elevator.

I recalled how a friend in Tokyo, who worked with people with disabilities, had said that the transportation system had become accessible only after officials realized how inconvenient the subway was for wheelchair users. If people like us didn't go out and show others how hard it was to get around, if we didn't make ourselves a burden, they could continue in oblivion. The staff of Le Jules Verne could ignore the inaccessibility of their restaurant. We had to do this for wheelchair users everywhere.

As we rose, we could see the Seine, the sky and the city splayed below. Lilia aimed my camera down, snapping photos of the metal struts.

The elevator door opened to a battalion of waiters bustling about. We were shown to our table, which, alas, was not next to the window, but we could still see the city beyond. I slid my feet out of the leopard-print heels — ahh! — and lined up my shoes and Lilia's under the table.

Our waiter appeared. *"En francais ou anglais?"* he demanded.

"En francais," I said. Why not? I had spent many years studying French as a college student and I needed

to put it to some use. Plus, speaking French made me feel sophisticated. And Lilia was so impressed.

The waiter offered to take our photo. Then he gave the camera back to Lilia, and she took a picture of the butter, then, the cheese puffs and my glass of Champagne, then the starter, something made with lentils and wasabi.

I tried to explain the significance of Jules Verne to Lilia. Admittedly, we had concentrated more on female figures in French history while preparing for our trip. But she'd watched the Jackie Chan version of "Around the World in 80 Days," and she'd gone on the "Journey to the Center of the Earth Ride" at Tokyo Disneyland, so I figured she had some idea.

Evening began to fall on Paris, and soon it was indeed the City of Lights.

Lilia took a photo of the asparagus in sabayon, which was fat and juicy, and from Provence.

I confess I'd been worried that the waiters and other diners would look askance at a child in a wheelchair, but the staff seemed charmed. When the bread basket came around for the second and third times, and Lilia indicated that she wanted more, I frowned. But the waiter, calling her "*la petite*," and "*Mademoiselle*," encouraged Lilia to help herself. Well, maybe she was being greedy, but at home we ate nothing but rice. We were in Paris — why not? City of Lights! City of Bread!

During the meat course, the Eiffel Tower began to sparkle — like the Champagne in my glass, like the sequins on my dress.

I told Lilia that it had been my dream to visit Paris with her since she was small.

"Really?" she asked. She loved hearing stories about her babyhood. She loved knowing that we'd had the same dream of Paris.

"Yes. When I learned that you couldn't walk, I wasn't sure if it was possible. But here we are!"

Moved, she wiped away a tear. "Thank you!" she signed.

By the time we'd finished the fish course, the meat course and two of three dessert courses (pistachio ice cream), three hours had passed and the lights on the tower had flickered two more times. We were stuffed to the gills. We couldn't finish the homemade marshmallows. Unbelievably, we left chocolate on the table. I'd read somewhere that the French didn't do doggy bags, but our waiter kindly offered to wrap up the remaining sweets for us to take back to our hotel.

When we were ready to go, I put my shoes back on and asked the hostess to call a taxi for us. As we got into our coats, she handed Lilia a couple of packages of madeleines, and chatted with me.

"Doesn't she speak?" she asked, noticing that I'd signed with Lilia.

"No," I said. "She's deaf."

Lilia wagged her finger. "*Nani? Nani?*" What? What?

I put my hand under my chin, meaning, "I'll tell you later."

The hostess and I talked about the differences between American and Japanese and French Sign Language. "Thank you" in ASL is about the same as "Bonjour" in French Sign Language, I'd discovered.

"It must be hard to get around," she said, referring to the wheelchair.

I told her that it was easier than I'd imagined. Although Paris was not altogether accessible, we had managed to cover quite a bit of ground. I was feeling proud of myself.

"Is it just the two of you?" she asked.

I wasn't sure if she was referring to the evening, or to our lives in general. Maybe she imagined that I was a single mom, struggling to raise my handicapped child alone. I didn't want her to think of us in that way.

I told her that we'd come alone, and that my husband and son stayed in Japan. "It was her dream to come to Paris," I said.

"And here you are."

"Yes, here we are."

"Bon courage," she said, when the elevator arrived. "Good luck!"

Lilia waved enthusiastically with one hand, gripping the bag of madeleines in the other, while I felt curiously deflated. We'd had a lovely dinner, but the hostess had gotten hung up on Lilia's disabilities. I didn't go around feeling sorry for myself, and I didn't want other people to pity me, or Lilia. I wanted them to see Lilia not as a deaf girl in a wheelchair, not as my inescapable burden, but as a well-rounded individual with a place in the world. She had a rich interior life. She had ideas and opinions. She was aware of things.

I wanted the taciturn elevator operator to understand this, too, which is why I said, "My daughter told me that there have been many suicides from the Eiffel Tower."

He made some vague noise. Obviously this was not suitable elevator conversation. My husband often said that I was incapable of "reading the air," and maybe he was right. Even so, I imagined that since he'd asked Tokyo Disneyland employees about the Day of the Earthquake, breaking the spell of the Magic Kingdom, he would have asked the same thing.

"But she said that precautions have been taken," I continued, "and that there aren't so many anymore."

"*Eh, voila,*" he replied.

We were silent the rest of the way down.

Later, back home in Japan, I did an Internet search for "suicide" and "Eiffel Tower" and discovered that it is indeed one of the most popular suicide sites in Europe.In fact, just the day before, a man "in John Lennon-style sunglasses and Bermuda shorts" had had to be talked off the ledge. An accompanying article reported, "Tower staff refuse to divulge the exact number of such incidents every year for fear of encouraging them."

Eh, voila!

On the way to the airport for our flight home, I listened to the radio. The announcer said that the previous evening, around the time that we would have been having our meat course, someone called in a bomb threat to the Eiffel Tower. More than 1,000 people were evacuated from the area. My mind flashed to an image of Lilia in her wheelchair and me, teetering on 4-inch leopard-print heels, trying to cram ourselves into the elevator like Titanic passengers rushing for the lifeboats. I cleared my head and sank back in the car seat, flooded with relief.

Lilia signed, "I want to come back!"

Suzanne Kamata is the author of three novels, including Losing Kei; Gadget Girl: The Art of Being Invisible, which was awarded the Asian Pacific American Librarians Association Honor for Young Adult Literature and named a Book of Outstanding Merit by Bank Street College, and Screaming Divas, which was named to the American Library Association's Rainbow List. She also is the author of the award-wining short story collection, The Beautiful One Has Come. She lives in Japan with her husband and teenage twins and teaches English as a foreign language at Tokushima University. She is an MFA candidate at the University of British Columbia.

SACRED ENCOUNTERS
Spain

More than two decades ago, while living and studying in Spain, I took a bus from Madrid to Granada on the day before Palm Sunday. I have made that trip many times since, but never so memorably as on that day when I shared my seat with a cloistered nun named Pilar.

She caught my eye the moment she boarded the bus, dressed in black wool clothes from head to toe — despite the April warmth. For luggage she carried an assortment of plastic bags. I was struck by the intensity of both her faith and her fear, the way she gripped her rosary with the panic of a small child and murmured again and again, "Blessed Virgin, protect me." As we pulled out of the station she crossed herself energetically, shut her eyes, and prayed. Her lips did not stop moving until we were on the highway heading south.

I had glimpsed such women before. In churches throughout Spain I had seen them hovering behind ornate iron grilles or drifting wordlessly in and out of chapel doors like ghosts. But I had never met one of these ethereal beings, had never sat beside one for seven hours on a public bus and tried to make conversation.

"*¡Qué calor!*" Pilar volunteered, once we'd left Madrid and the city's concrete towers had given way to green fields and herds of sheep. She shielded her face from the sun. Where the white band of her headdress cut into her forehead, her pink skin glistened with sweat. She must have been in her late 50s, I thought, trying not to stare. But she was staring, too. "*Americana?*" she asked with a hopeful smile.

"Yes," I said.

"Ahhh."

We rode past hills scored with vineyards, past faded Castilian villages. Pilar told me her name and explained that she was traveling from a cloistered convent in Madrid to one in Granada, where she had lived many years ago, to assume the post of Mother Superior. Granada was her birthplace — she ached to see the city again.

Emboldened by her candor, I asked about convent life. It's a quiet existence, she answered, and a pretty one. But not without its drawbacks. In Madrid her convent had no heat, and she slept under five blankets in the winter. She wore wool year-round, even in summer, and always stockings. The order required it. Yes, her habit was hot, and yes, the fabric around her face bothered her.

As she talked, she fumbled beneath the black layers of her habit for her rosary. From time to time she gazed out the window and prayed.

We talked about the Holy Week processions we would both witness the following week in Granada, Pilar for the first time in years, I for the first time in my life. Because I was in Spain to research a biography of Granadan poet Federico García Lorca — who once marched barefoot in a Good Friday procession — I was keen to see this timeless Andalusian pageant, where poly-chromed figures of Christ and the Virgin Mary are paraded through the city's streets on the backs of peni-tents. Pilar told me about her own convent's Virgin, "*La Inmaculada*," whom they would robe in blue and trim with candles and flowers on Holy Thursday night. She spoke as though describing a beloved daughter.

In La Mancha we stopped at a gas station for lunch. Pilar and I stood together beneath the shade of a tree, away from the other passengers. From one of her plastic bags she produced a sandwich, two meat pies, two car-tons of juice, an orange and a banana. She fished a small knife from the voluminous pockets of her habit and briskly sliced pieces of fruit into my hands. Briefly she lowered her head in prayer. I did the same, mouthing words I had learned in my Episcopalian childhood, mar-veling at the way the people and places we meet on the road can return us to our past.

We ate in silence, then boarded the bus and resumed our journey. Late that afternoon, as we entered Andalusia, Pilar put her hand to her chest and sighed. When we reached Granada, she squeezed my arm. We said good-bye; I promised to visit.

At dusk the next night, Palm Sunday, the first hooded penitents emerged from one of Granada's many churches, bearing a huge platform topped with candles, carnations and life-sized wooden figures arranged in a scene from the Passion of Christ. Each night from then until Easter the spectacle was the same: long parades of penitents, some of them barefoot, carrying crosses, candles, drums and towering scenes from Christ's Passion through the streets. And polychromed Virgins. I had never seen so many Virgins before, each one draped in yards of embroidered fabric, each one pale with grief, a jeweled teardrop suspended on her cheek.

On Thursday night Pilar's Virgin swept onto the streets, dressed in pale blue as promised. On Friday night the gypsies brought out their Mary, clothed in pure black. By Saturday I had witnessed the whole of Christ's murder played out in its various stages and had seen so many weeping Virgins I felt publicly implicated in the crime. Easter came as a relief.

On Easter afternoon I made my way to Pilar's convent. The immense yellow building consumed the better part of a city block. I rang a bell and was told by a dis-embodied voice hidden behind a door to enter. In the foyer a sign read, "This is the house of the Mother of God." From behind another locked door the invisible voice steered me to a small cupboard in the wall; it turned out to conceal a kind of shuttered lazy-Susan. I yanked on a chain, the contraption turned, and a large brass key appeared. The voice instructed me to proceed to an adjoining door and unlock it.

Inside, Pilar stood on the far side of an iron grille that divided a room scattered with furniture. She pushed her hands through the narrow bars to greet me. I felt as though I were in a zoo. We sat down in silk-covered chairs on either side of the divider. A plastic infant Jesus lay on a pillow in front of Pilar's knees.

I did not stay long. Pilar offered me a thick wedge of fried pastry dusted heavily with powdered sugar and packed with sweet potato, a convent specialty. "Delicious," I said, struggling to wipe the sugar from my face. I told her about the processions I had seen that week.

"Ah," she said. "Their beauty fills the soul."
I nodded.

She asked if I knew anyone in America who might like to join her convent. "We are only seven," she said sadly.

No, I knew of no one.

"Not you? she asked.

For an instant I tried to picture myself living on the other side of those bars. I smiled and shook my head.
Soon it was time to go; Mass would begin shortly. Pilar suggested I might like to see the convent garden before I left, and abruptly opened a door onto the patio. A sudden perfume, intensely sweet, filled the room. I could see sunlit benches and paths, and everywhere pendulous lav-

ender flowers — wisteria, the source of that overpowering fragrance. I had not expected such splendor. Pilar reached into her pocket for her knife and clipped a bloom for me. "*Un recuerdo*," she said.

*****

We saw each other once more that year, at Christmas, and then I left Spain, We did not see each other again until I returned to Granada eight years later for a brief visit and one evening retraced my steps to her convent. Although I had thought of Pilar often over the years, we had not written, and I wondered if she would remember me. Or had I merely been a curiosity to her, as she first was to me?

I knocked on the familiar door. An invisible voice responded. I gave my name and said I wished to see Pilar. The voice mumbled something about Mass and told me to wait. As I did, three gypsy children rushed into the foyer, stinking of urine and begging money and food. I gave them each a coin.

This time there was no turntable, no key, simply a door that abruptly opened and on the other side of it Pilar, smiling broadly and reaching toward me with her hands. She waved me inside and we sat opposite each other in a small room, no divider. She was full of questions. How was I? And where? Was I still single? With unaccustomed embarrassment I told her I had been married and divorced since we'd last met. Well, she reflected, these things happen. This time there was no mention of my joining the convent. But perhaps I would like to see the chapel?

The convent watchdog, a small terrier, followed us down the long hall to the chapel and waited patiently beside the altar while Pilar showed me the sanctuary. She muttered tiny prayers as she led me from one statue to another. Here is St. James, she said. Our patron. And here is the Mother of God. "*Madre mía.*" And here, she said, pointing to the life-size polychromed Virgin I had seen paraded through the streets eight years earlier, is *La Inmaculada.* "*Santísima, santísima.*" I felt a strange rush of affection. "Their beauty fills the soul," Pilar had said of Granada's Holy Week processions. It was true of Pilar herself, I thought. Of the whole, fantastic world she inhabited.

To the rear of the chapel, on the far side of an iron grille, stood a half-dozen young Indian women in black habits, praying. "*Novitiates,*" Pilar whispered. "We are 15 now. They are beginning to learn Spanish."

Before saying goodbye she handed me an ironstone jar stamped with the red cross of St. James and filled with cherry preserves — another convent specialty. At the door to the street we encountered the gypsy children. "They come every day," Pilar sighed. "But if we don't feed them, who will?"

She motioned for the children to go around the corner, and through the bars of a side window she handed them a small loaf of bread. The children squealed. As I turned to leave I saw them fling their hands over their heads, as though holding castanets. They began to dance.

Leslie Stainton is the author of "Lorca: A Dream of Life" (Bloomsbury, 1998; Farrar Straus Giroux, 1999) and "Staging Ground" (Penn State University Press, 2014). Her essays and articles have appeared in The New York Times and Washington Post travel sections, Michigan Quarterly Review, Memoir, River Teeth, Crab Orchard Review, Brevity, and elsewhere. She is an editor at the University of Michigan, where she also has taught creative nonfiction, and is a past creative nonfiction fellow at the Prague Summer Writers Workshop.

THE PHYSICAL
China

It's been two weeks since I've arrived in China to teach second-year students composition at an English-medium university. My days have literally turned to nights and my nights to days. Now, I am to undergo a physical examination — a requirement for all foreign employees. So, 8 a.m. Wednesday finds me on my way to the university, venturing up a steep hill through a curtain of humidity that could rival a Swedish sauna.

I am to meet Ms. Liu, the associate dean's administrative assistant, who will accompany me to my appointment. Along the way, mountains rise regally against a faint blue morning sky and old people practice tai chi in a dilapidated basketball court. Feral cats dart in and out of unevenly trimmed hedges, and a song emanates out of public loud speakers atop tall wooden posts, the singer's screech so high that it threatens the strength of store shop windows.

Ms. Lui spots me and offers the slightest wave of her hand. In return, I offer half-a-windshield-wiper wave. Upon reaching her, she asks if I remembered not to eat breakfast. As I have been unable to tolerate even a cracker upon arrival, I assure her that I have not eaten.
8:04 a.m.

Mr. Wu arrives with the school shuttle. I climb into the back seat with nary a frayed seat belt to hold me in place in case one of the many city buses or honking taxis should collide with us. Fifteen minutes later and a new understanding of traffic signals as mere suggestions, Mr. Wu pulls in front of a high-rise that houses, among other enterprises, a clinic.
8:20 a.m.

I follow Ms. Liu across the institutional shiny green lobby to an elevator where a melee has broken out. People shove and push and enter and exit while the poor elevator doors try to do their job. Ms. Liu, no shrinking violet, pushes me into the melee, and it is here that I, too, learn not to be a shrinking violet, for I might suffer the unfortunate fate of falling down and becoming trampled upon. As I shoulder my way to the elevator doors with Ms. Liu in my wake, my mind desperately searches for a past experience to make sense of this chaos, and calls up fourth grade school recess.

Fifth floor — our stop. Thoughts of pushy children on monkey bars quickly disappear and are replaced with scenes from old hospital drama TV shows. White paper hats adorn the nurses' heads. I suppress the urge to snicker. Ms. Liu walks to a counter and hands my papers to a nurse who proceeds to vigorously stamp every page, sometimes more than once. With arm lifted halfway in air followed by a swift downward stroke, the stamper is jammed into red ink and then lands with a clean thud onto the paper. Jam, thud, thud, thud, flip, jam, thud, thud, thud. The slightest lift in the corners of the nurse's mouth betrays her stern countenance when performing this most officious of acts.

8:31 a.m.

Papers returned to Ms. Liu, we sit in a row of connected chairs one would find at a bus terminal. A minute later — is that possible? — my name is called. I follow Ms. Liu down a short hall with little rooms on either side fitted with white curtains on metal rods for doors. She stops in front of one, yanks it open and departs. The nurse inside beckons me forth.

First, my blood pressure is checked. If, dear reader, you should desire a similar experience, may I suggest visiting your local drugstore. As I sit and slide my arm through a machine that will soon fill with air and tenderly squeeze it, I half expect the nurse to drop a coin into the machine's slot. Instead, she presses a button — a perk to be sure. After recording my blood pressure, she motions for me to face her and lift my shirt. Oops, the curtain is open. With an apologetic smile to the American who is accustomed to privacy, she pulls it closed.

Back on her stool, she motions again. I lift my shirt, and she pulls out a stethoscope. Now, I am to lift my bra as well. Hmmm, I think as I feel the press of cold steel against my skin. I'm not aware that my heart is located next to my left nipple. Now my right nipple. Back to the other breast, this time the left side. She gestures for me to stand. I rise, stuffing my American breasts back into my bra and then pull down my shirt just in time for her to usher me into the next room, where a young man is assisting an old man off an examination table.

They exit the room, and a technician indicates for me to lie down on the table and pull up my shirt. What this time, I wonder, as she holds up metal clips with wires dangling from them. The clips are soon affixed to my chest, legs and ankles. But I move too fast in my narrative, for she first swabs me with water, using what looks to be a tired remnant of a once porous and plump sea sponge. After the clips, she straps down my wrists . . . and this, dear reader, is where the story of my life ends, for I am about to be electrocuted.

Or, so I think. With heart palpitating and palms sweating, I watch nervously as the technician positions herself behind a machine that before long unrolls a long white tongue of tape. One can hazard a guess that they are stock quotes. She tears off the tongue and clips it to my papers, and soon I am unfettered and shuffled to the X-ray room, where an impatient assistant pushes me in front of an X-ray machine for a chest X-ray.

I explain to him, in hopes that he understands English, that I am wearing an underwire bra that contains metal. He waves off my concern as one would swat a bothersome fly. My apprehension having not been eased, I fetch Ms. Liu to translate. After what appears to be two seconds of exchanges, not enough time as far I am concerned to explain the situation, Ms. Liu turns to me and says, "No problem. Leave bra on." Standing in front of the machine holding a protective apron behind me, I subtract five years from my life.

8:51 a.m.

I am in a white room with a nurse giving me the thumbs-up. Actually, she is gesturing to a chart with her thumb up: Thumbs-up means "E" is on its back. Thumbs-down designates an "E" with its backbone on top while a thumbs-east indicates an eastwardly facing "E" and thumbs-west indicates a westwardly facing "E." Please forgive me, dear reader, if you should find me a braggart, but I surpassed my own expectations at this eye exam, for I was forbidden to wear my spectacles. Furthermore, I was allowed to complete this exam without having to lift my shirt.

What I now present is not as horrific as it sounds. The next phase of my examination entails a blood test. My veins are visible and near the surface, always a genuine delight to those poor, overworked lab assistants in the U.S. However, these same veins, according the young assistant sitting across from me, transmogrified into fearsome low-laying veins, not unlike bottom feeders.

With the vigor of Chinese stamping, she at once slaps and pokes my arm with her finger. Slap, slap, slap, poke, poke, poke, shake of head, slap, slap, slap, poke, poke, poke. What soon spreads across her face is not dissimilar to the smile found on Alice's Cheshire cat. She uncaps a suspiciously large needle. I gulp. The assistant, though, painlessly and expertly slips it under my skin and into my vein. Two vials-worth later and none the worse for wear, I am propelled to the next stage of my Chinese physical examination.

9:02 a.m.

Another room, another table, another technician. Lying down, I once again am instructed to lift my shirt, a course of action that now feels second nature. I muse whether upon meeting Chinese people in the future if I shall instinctively lift my shirt in salutation.

My musings end abruptly by a sudden squirt of cold lubricant onto my skin. The technician shoves a transducer probe between my ribcage and expeditiously glides it to the left and then over to the right as she examines the images on the monitor. Apparently not satisfied, she pushes down harder on the probe, such pressure as one would use when scooping out frozen ice cream. With each drive home of the probe, I imagine black and blue flowers preparing to bloom on my skin. Upon completion, the technician plucks tissue from a box and proceeds to clean the probe with great care. The probe cleaned to her satisfaction, she hands me the very same tissue with which to clean myself.

9:13 a.m.

I soon re-join Ms. Liu in the waiting area where we commence at once toward the elevator, which will bring me to the last stage of my physical examination. During those few claustrophobic moments in the elevator where I witness grown men insert their fingers up their nostrils and stir about with the earnestness of stamping papers, I find it curious that I have neither been weighed nor measured.

Anon, the doors part to present a scene one might witness at a busy airport. Instead of hurrying to and fro to check luggage and catch planes, these people are most eager to acquire their urine cups and vials. Having attained mine, I make my way to the toilets and search for an empty stall. After I find one and close the door, I reach to turn the lock. No lock. The crackling air of activity just on the other side of this unlocked door encourages me to hastily produce urine. After pulling down my jeans and underwear, I cautiously squat over the hole, not wanting to accidentally step in it or urinate outside of it or on my clothes.

Positioned appropriately, I strategically hold beneath me a cup the size of those small paper containers used for mints and peanuts at weddings. I take a few breaths and relax. As my bladder relinquishes a few drops of precious urine, the door opens. "Someone is in here," I yell in English, trying not to sound frantic. The door closes. Not a drop lost. With concentration akin to a nuclear scientist's, I pour the contents of the cup into the vial. Where to throw away the cup? Oh, where everyone else has — on top of the empty toilet paper holder, so I place mine gingerly into another cup that still contains urine.

Holding the vial in one hand, I maneuver my hips back and forth as my other hand alternates between sides, inching up first my underwear and then jeans. Droplets of urine clinging to me get absorbed into my white cotton underwear — a most uncomfortable feeling. A one-handed button and zip of my jeans as smooth as a teenage boy's practiced hand on a girl's bra, I exit the stall and enter the fray holding my vial before me like a lit memorial candle and place it in a holding tray with the others. No stoppers needed on these soldiers of urine standing at attention, only a uniform number. I make my way back through a throng of people to wash my hands at one of the two empty faucets in the hectic toilet area.

While lathering a new bar of soap, I notice a dirty mop, mop side up, resting against the wall next to a pail of dirty water. When I finish washing, I reach for a cloth towel hanging from a hook within touching distance of the mop. Uneasiness settles about me as I wonder how many days, weeks, that towel has been hanging there. I quell my anxieties by remembering that I am in China, where hand washing is as foreign as free speech.

9:24 a.m.

My physical examination officially complete, Ms. Liu and I exit the high-rise and wait outside in the mid-morning smog for the shuttle. "Hungry?" she asks. "No," I respond as scenes from my physical examination rise like a specter before me.

On the way back to the university, I think about my students whose Chinese names I wish to learn. They insist on being called by the American names they had chosen, however, common names like Glitter and Snow and, for one male student, Flower. Yet, I also think that my students' American names might reflect their understanding of American culture through the lens of their culture, where their Chinese names can also mean the names of things.

I, too, dear reader have used my cultural lens to translate my visit to the clinic this morning and will continue to use that lens for the many new experiences that await me in my host country. We will have to provide latitude and an appreciation for difference, my students and I, as we both negotiate each other's traditional landscapes. It is an intercultural dance that I will treasure for years to come.

Jill Boyles' work has appeared in Toasted Cheese, The Ilanot Review, and Calliope Magazine, among other publications. She holds a MFA in writing from Hamline University. She was the recipient of a Minnesota State Arts Board grant and a finalist for the Jerome Grant.

A BLESSING
Bangladesh

The year was 1986 and I was 18. The country was Bangladesh. My Asian destinations were to be Mount Everest Base Camp followed by the beaches of Thailand. Bangladesh wasn't a part of my plan, and the airline's two-day layover in Dhaka seemed like a scheme to profit from the Western tourist trade that otherwise would have passed the country by. I knew nothing about Bangladesh, nothing of its recent independence from Pakistan, military coups and martial law, or of the largely Islamic population.

Arriving at the airport, our small group of tourists was herded together — in an embarrassing fashion given that we were all the sort of seasoned travelers who would normally try to avoid each other so as not to stick out in an exotic country. But there we were, huddled together, our pasty skin gleaming with sweat, wearing drab colors, and cameras dangling.

Swarthy locals swarmed the single gate and terminal in an aggressive mass, hollering at one another. They were all men. I realized immediately that my European summer beach clothes, the wrap-around skirt, tank top and sandals exposing my ankles and toes, were not appropriate dress in a Muslim country. My blonde hair flowing freely down my back only added to my predicament.

And so it began: gropes, squeezes and pinches to my ass, small breasts and skinny arms; tugs at my bony wrists. Any exposed skin, however meager, was fair game to pawing as the crowd followed us out to the rickety, exhaust-fuming mini-bus waiting at the curb. I knew then that I couldn't count on my two traveling companions. They became frightened boys who pretended not to see hands reaching out of nowhere, like the multiple arms of a Hindu god, to feel up their ill-fated female friend. I felt humiliated, and I knew I was on my own.

We were driven to the only Western hotel in Dhaka — its sole function to baby-sit the tourists during the forced two-day layover. We were ordered, or at least told firmly, not to leave the hotel, which, of course, I ignored. And yet, I had not been prepared to walk out onto the streets of Dhaka. Bangladesh was poor in a way I had never seen, even during my travels into remote areas of Central America.

Whereas the airport had belonged to men, the streets of Dhaka belonged to women and children, who trudged along muddy, monsoon-washed streets laced with animal remains, raw sewage and bloodsucking leeches dropped there by the torrential rains. Everything was filthy, redolent of decay, and the humidity was suffocating. The only sign of gaiety was in the vibrant colors of the saris that some of the women wore.

I stepped on a bloated, dead rat and shuddered. Beggars swarmed me, and I had to push through a crowd as I made my way back to the safe haven of the hotel. There I sat in the dining room eating vegetable curry, everything covered in a thin film of grease, including myself. The hotel didn't provide drinking water, so I had cup after cup of hot chai, sipped in the stifling heat.

I hated to admit that I was scared. I also hated to admit that I didn't like Bangladesh with its groping men and muddy, noisy streets. I wanted to believe I was a world traveler and that I was intrepid. Truthfully, I was relieved when it was time to board the mini-bus that would take us back to the airport.

I sat on the bus and leaned against the half-open window while we waited for the driver. The engine rattled in neutral. I looked out at the tropical landscape surrounding the hotel, and then I noticed an old woman standing below the window. As we made eye contact, she reached her hand up toward me in that familiar gesture of the beggars. The outstretched hand and her self-conscious smile saddened me. I knew all the good reasons not to give money to beggars; I couldn't help feeling embarrassed, for myself and for her. She was begging, but I could tell that was not her usual custom.

I examined her more carefully. She appeared ancient, shrunken and pruned, with her silvery hair set in a dignified bun. Her purple sari was worn and faded. She was barefoot and toothless. I was done for; she wasn't going to leave me alone now that she caught me contemplating her. She nodded, smiled and persisted with the outstretched hand, cupped just beneath the window. I smiled back, shook my head apologetically and squirmed in my seat.

Thoughts ran through my mind: She must think I am a cheap American who won't even spare small change for an old lady. She smiles at me, but she really must hate me. Maybe she will put some sort of curse on me.

All the while I smiled, nodded and squirmed. Where in the hell was that bus driver?

The driver finally climbed onto the bus. Just before we pulled out, I saw the old woman dash off and she was out of sight. Again, I was relieved. A few minutes later, the engine revved and I could feel the pull and sway of the bus as we began to move. But then something caught my eye. The old woman was slowly running alongside my window, and she reached up and tossed something inside.

It happened in slow motion. Dozens of small, brilliant magenta, yellow and red flowers showered me. Delicate and colorful flowers were everywhere. They stuck to my hair and my blouse. They covered my lap and the seat around me. I had been doused with a brilliance of color and the sweet scent of a garden.

I leaned my head out as we drove away and I saw the old woman smiling and waving joyfully. I waved back. She had blessed me with flowers, and I wasn't scared anymore.

Claire is a writer, poet, and photographer. She was a contributor to Adventures of a Lifetime: Travel Tales from Around the World by World Traveler Press in 2015. Her work has appeared in other fine journals and anthologies, including The MacGuffin, Sliver of Stone, Boston Literary Magazine, and An Honest Lie. Claire is currently in the MFA creative writing program at Florida International University.

CREDITS

"The Human Race" by Bernadette Murphy, published with permission of the author. Copyright © 2015 by Bernadette Murphy

"A Walk in the Woods" by Katie Hammel, published with permission of the author. Copyright © 2014 by Katie Hammel

"Stars and a Stranger" by Nadine Michèle Payn, published with permission of the author. Copyright © 2003 by Nadine Michèle Payn

"Thailand's Lost Children" by Janna Graber, published with permission of the author. Copyright © 2015 by Janna Graber

"Travel Charades" by Mary Ann Sternberg, published with permission of the author. Copyright © 2014 by Mary Ann Sternberg

ACKNOWLEDGMENTS

Thanks again to former Denver Post Travel Editor Mim Swartz for your editing expertise and advice. It's always a pleasure!

A huge thank you to my mom and dad for letting me tromp off to Europe my junior year, and for supporting me and my dreams, even when they didn't always make sense.

And to my kids and sweetheart, Ben, thanks for all your patience, support and understanding while I worked on yet another book. Having you in my life is my greatest joy.

WORLD TRAVELER TALES
---

*Chance Encounters: Travel Tales from Around the
World* (World Traveler Press, 2014)

*Adventures of a Lifetime: Travel Tales from Around the
World* (World Traveler Press, 2015)

A Pink Suitcase: 22 Tales of Women's Travel
(World Traveler Press, 2015)

CPSIA information can be obtained at www.ICGtesting.com
Printed in the USA
BVOW11s1641071115

425657BV00001B/8/P